TRUE CRIME STORIES
of WESTERN
NORTH CAROLINA

TRUE CRIME STORIES of WESTERN NORTH CAROLINA

CATHY PICKENS

THE
History
PRESS

Published by The History Press
Charleston, SC
www.historypress.com

Cover images: Back, top left, view east from Clingmans Dome. *Acroterion, Wikimedia Commons*; back, bottom, Jumpinoff Rock. *Pmuellr, flickr.com*; front, top, near Newfound Gap. *Jim R. Rogers, flickr.com*; front, bottom, Popcorn Sutton. *Neal Hutcheson*; headlines from the *Charlotte Observer*.

First published 2022

Manufactured in the United States

ISBN 9781467152150

Library of Congress Control Number: 2022937926

Notice: The information in this book is true and complete to the best of our knowledge. It is offered without guarantee on the part of the author or The History Press. The author and The History Press disclaim all liability in connection with the use of this book.

Always, for those with stories to tell…and those who want to listen.

CONTENTS

ACKNOWLEDGEMENTS

Again, this book—and so many wonderful things in my life—wouldn't have happened without other writers, researchers, librarians, historians, journalists and those who've investigated and preserved these stories. I owe special thanks to the following:

Keith Vincent and his Courthouse History website (http://courthousehistory. com), which helps me double-check which courthouse hosted a particular trial. It's an invaluable and interesting resource.

Georgette Penland Shelton at Penland & Son's Department Store in Marshall. With her stories of playing with Nancy Morgan's kittens and of her mother serving on the jury, she reminded me that those not from a mountain community might not understand how close everything is—and how long are the memories.

Paula Connolly and E. Dickinson for their valuable feedback on these stories.

Highland's Stuart Ferguson, book lover and bookseller extraordinaire, for sharing his energy and stories.

Neal Hutcheson and his chronicling of Popcorn Sutton's life, as well as Reita Pendry, who first told me about the Ore Knob Mine.

Kate Jenkins, Jonny Foster, Ryan Finn and the amazing team at The History Press, which produces beautiful books to share these North Carolina stories.

And always, thanks to Bob, who is along for every adventure.

WELCOME

In 1663, what became North Carolina and South Carolina started as a land grant that ran from the Atlantic to the Pacific Oceans, presented by King Charles II of England to eight Lords Proprietor, the friends who had helped him become king.

In the end, the boundary-drawers reduced the ambitious grant and set the farthest reaches along the Appalachian mountain ridges. Later, Carolina was divided into what became two states because the settled coastal regions of North Carolina were a far journey from the seat of government in Charleston.

Dividing the states in some other configuration might have made more sense, given how much Western North Carolina differs from Eastern North Carolina in heritage, culture and foodways. In the central region of both Carolinas, rivers become less navigable and thick pine barrens formed a natural barrier between the coast and the mountains, which slowed inland settlement. But by the mid-1700s, English, Scotch-Irish and German settlers were moving into Western North Carolina from the coast and the Piedmont or from Pennsylvania and Maryland, making their homes where the land looked like the old country to many of them.

Today, Western North Carolina includes mountains and foothills, the unique city of Asheville, plenty of small towns and vast stretches of rugged national parks and rural farms. The land and those who settled it are distinctly different from the coastal areas or the more densely settled and

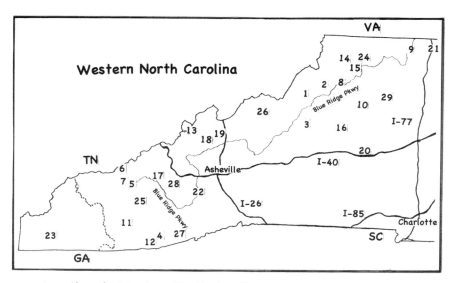

Locations in Western North Carolina

—————— Blue Ridge Parkway
. . . . . Appalachian Trail
▬▬▬▬ Interstate highways

1 Beech Mountain
2 Boone
3 Brown Mountain
4 Cashiers
5 Cherokee
6 Clingmans Dome & Newfound Gap
7 Deep Creek trailhead
8 Deep Gap
9 Dividing Ridge & Saddle Mtn Church
10 Dula & Foster graves/Wilkes Co.
11 Franklin/Macon County
12 Highlands
13 Hot Springs
14 Jefferson/Ashe County
15 Jumpinoff Place
16 Lenoir
17 Maggie Valley
18 Marshall/Madison County
19 Mars Hill
20 Morganton
21 Mount Airy
22 Mount Pisgah
23 Murphy
24 Ore Knob Mine
25 Sylva & Great Smokies Rwy
26 Toe River Valley & Silver grave
27 Toxaway Falls
28 Waynesville/Haywood County
29 Wilkesboro/Wilkes County

business-focused cities in the Piedmont. Western North Carolina attracts tourists and retirees with its natural beauty, but those who've called this home for generations were individualists bound to the land. The blending makes for some interesting stories…and interesting crimes.

Given the remoteness of much of this section of the state, the stories in this book naturally include plenty of those who went missing or cases that went unsolved, along with tales of modern-day moonshiners, old-fashioned

Looking Glass Falls, north of Brevard on Highway 276. *Courtesy of Hugo Andrew on Unsplash.com.*

Madison County Courthouse in Marshall. *Photo by Cathy Pickens.*

murder ballads, motorcycle gangs, not one but two bombings in the town called Mayberry and crimes that made headlines around the world.

My family has been in the Carolinas for more than three hundred years. Because any telling naturally depends on the storyteller's choices, these are cases that, for one reason or another, captured my imagination.

This book is not a work of investigative journalism. The information is drawn solely from published or broadcast resources—newspapers, television documentaries, podcasts, books, scholarly papers, print and online magazine articles. One of the drawbacks in recounting historical events is that accounts vary. Some reported "facts" aren't accurate, or they're at odds with someone else's memory or perception of the event. While I have worked to dig out as many points of view as I could find, I'm sure there are mistakes. My apologies in advance.

For me, what fascinates is not random violence, but rather people, their lives and their relationships. Some of these stories could have happened anywhere. Some made huge headlines far away from North Carolina. Others remain writ large mostly in the hearts of the family and friends of those involved.

The stories, woven together, demonstrate the rich variety of those who call this part of the state home. These are stories that have helped shape Western North Carolina. People and their pasts matter here. The stories are worth remembering, even when they involve loss and especially when they are tempered with affection and fond memories.

Welcome to Western North Carolina and its crime stories.

THE MAYBERRY BOMBINGS

The approach to the North Carolina mountains begins in gentle hills before the steeper climb to higher elevations. The views of the mountains and their changing shades of blue are one of the treats of living in the small towns nestled in the foothills.

Mount Airy is one of those small towns—although it is better known by another name. When *The Andy Griffith Show* debuted in 1960, Mayberry quickly became thought of as what an idyllic small southern town should look like. Devoted fans know that the TV town was patterned after Griffith's hometown of Mount Airy. Decades later, some residents still call their hometown Mayberry. A vintage Ford Galaxie police car cruises the streets, and Snappy Lunch, Floyd's Barber Shop and a replica jail invite tourists to stay and visit a while.

Mayberry is the last place anyone would expect a deadly bombing, but Mount Airy has seen not one but two separate lovelorn bombers.

By 1936, Dr. Harvey Richard Hege had been a Mount Airy dentist for a quarter of a century. On the side, he was also working to develop a new denture composite in a lab just over the Virginia line. Attractive Elsie Dickerson Salmons served as his receptionist for three years, although the older, married doctor's unwanted attentions made working with him awkward at times. When she announced her engagement to Curry Thomas, a wealthy farmer from Cape Charles on Virginia's Chesapeake Bay, Dr. Hege's obsession took a threatening turn. He sent letters and special-delivery

 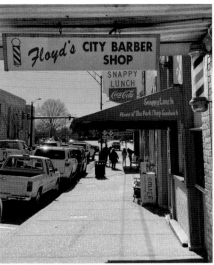

Left: A replica of the patrol car from TV's Mayberry still cruises the streets of Mount Airy. *Photo by Cathy Pickens.*

Right: Viewed from Main Street in Mount Airy, Dr. Hege's home once stood just past the post office (the large white building on the left). *Photo by Cathy Pickens.*

telegrams telling her not to leave, not to get married. In language familiar to domestic violence victims, he said that if he couldn't have her, no one could.

Elsie had been married and divorced from John Salmons, who lived in Virginia. Curry had also been married; his first wife was killed in a train wreck. The two felt fortunate to have found another chance at life and love. Ignoring Hege's odd and obsessive messages, Elsie, thirty-five, and Curry, forty-seven, married on June 10 at her mother's home in Virginia, and they moved to the Virginia coast to settle at Cape Charles, in Curry's late eighteenth-century home.

On July 22, just weeks after their wedding, the newlyweds played an afternoon round of golf and then stopped by the post office on their way home to pick up a package. The Richmond postmark suggested a wedding gift from Curry's father. The postal workers wanted them to open it there, but the couple decided to savor the surprise until they got home.

Curry pulled in their driveway and, before he even got out of the car, began unwrapping the package. Elsie had already stepped onto the running board on the passenger side when she heard a *click*, like a mousetrap. The loud explosion attracted nearby farm workers, who found Elsie thrown a distance from the car and unconscious. She was badly injured but survived. The blast had blown Curry through the roof and away from the car, killing him instantly. Car parts were scattered several yards around the wreckage.

Despite their destructive force, bombs invariably leave clues to their components. Two federal postal inspectors sent from Baltimore to investigate—B.B. Webb and J.B. Sentman—hoped those clues would lead to the bomb maker. Among the debris, they found a battery label, part of the mailing label and the mousetrap-like mechanism that snapped to form the connection that detonated it.

The investigators eliminated the first logical suspects, particularly Elsie's ex-husband. He was in Virginia and suffered from a brain injury that often hospitalized him. He likely wasn't able to construct such a plot, nor did he have a reason. No one in Cape Charles seemed to have a motive either. The focus soon turned to Dr. Hege. After all, he hadn't been very subtle about his feelings or his threats.

The federal investigators were thorough. They traced the battery label from the Canadian manufacturer to a Cleveland distributor to a Mount Airy hardware store. Before "buy local" was a byword, the bomber had stayed close to home, also buying string and two sticks of dynamite in town, as well as a short length of pipe and pipe caps from a local plumbing store. The typeface on the mailing label led to a Chicago manufacturer and then to the identifiable quirks unique to the typewriter in Dr. Hege's office.

From the materials collected, investigators were able to mock up a package like the one that contained the bomb. When the postal inspectors showed it to workers at the facilities that would have handled the package, one clerk described the man who mailed it, giving a good description of Dr. Hege. They learned that Dr. Hege and his friend Ed Banner had conveniently been in Richmond the day the package was mailed.

The federal agents wanted to keep the case in Virginia, where the bombing occurred, and avoid the need for extradition proceedings, so they arranged for a woman to lure Hege and Banner across the state line into Virginia, maybe with promises of a liaison at the Bluemont Hotel. The two men were arrested on Monday evening, October 5, and driven across the state to Virginia's Eastern Shore.

Just hours after they placed Hege in his cell, a sharp-eyed jailer spotted blood trickling under the door. When they unlocked his cell, Hege claimed that the bloody injury to his wrist was an accidental cut from his wristwatch, although he wasn't wearing one—he carried a pocket watch. A local doctor stitched his wound, and the jailers kept an even closer eye on him.

Right: Dr. Hege operated his dental practice in the office above the hardware store. *Photo by Cathy Pickens.*

Below: Dr. Hege donated the land for the God's Acre Cemetery at Grace Moravian Church. *Photo by Cathy Pickens.*

When Dr. Hege's wife and his lawyer drove from Mount Airy to visit him, he swore to her that he had nothing to do with the bombing. Before his visitors left Virginia to return to Mount Airy, his wife asked if the jailers would return his glasses so he could read the newspapers. Instead of reading, Hege used the glasses to cut an artery in his wrist and his jugular vein—or, as the *Suffolk News-Herald* reported, he "slaughtered" his neck and wrist. To avoid the blood trail that had alerted the jailer earlier in the week, one account said he let the blood flow into his suitcase. Early the next morning, on Sunday, October 11, he was found dead, lying on his cot.

Dr. Hege was buried three days later, on October 14, at Mount Airy's Grace Moravian Cemetery on North Main Street, on land he'd donated for God's Acre.

Banner, descendant of one of Mount Airy's founding families and a longtime friend of Dr. Hege, was released from jail in Virginia and not prosecuted once the commonwealth's attorney was convinced that Banner didn't know the real purpose of their trip to Richmond.

ANOTHER BOMBING

One deadly bombing originating in a small town would be noteworthy enough, but on New Year's Eve 1951, another bomb exploded, this one in the parking area at Mount Airy's Franklin Apartments. Twenty-four-year-old William H. Cochrane, a popular teacher at White Plains School, had climbed into his pickup truck for the start of classes after Christmas break. His wife, Imogene Moses Cochrane, had already left their apartment for her job at the Surry County Home Extension Office. The two had been married only four months.

William turned the ignition. Years later, a newspaper reporter at the *Mount Airy News* remembered feeling the blast blocks away at the newspaper office. Windows shattered in the apartment building. The blast blew William through the truck's roof; he landed a dozen feet away but was still alive and able to speak to those who ran to help him.

In an attempt to save his life, doctors at the hospital amputated both legs. A deputy stayed outside his room, in case the attacker made another attempt. William died thirteen hours after the blast.

An estimated three thousand people filed through Moody's Funeral Home in Mount Airy for the visitation. The funeral was held four hours away in William's hometown of Franklin, where his father was the police chief.

A lovelorn bombing attack occurred outside Mount Airy's Franklin Apartments. *Photo by Cathy Pickens.*

The Mount Airy police chief personally carried the bomb components to the Federal Bureau of Investigation lab in Washington. The City of Mount Airy offered a $2,500 reward; Governor Kerr Scott added $400 to the pot. Local police and agents from North Carolina's State Bureau of Investigation (SBI) came to Mount Airy to interview everyone in William's life. Who had a grudge against William Cochrane? Did anyone wish him ill? Had there been any altercations lately? Did this have something to do with his father's job as police chief in Macon County?

They kept digging into the background of both William and his wife, Imogene, including anyone she dated while attending Appalachian State Teacher's College and while living in Chatham County at her first teaching job. For more than two years, they asked questions but unearthed no solid leads.

About a year after the murder, the young widow moved across the state to Edenton, North Carolina, to restart her life. In April 1954, after living in Eastern North Carolina about two years, Imogene was making wedding plans. George Byrum, who served on the city council and was "one of Edenton's most eligible bachelors," had asked her to marry him. She had given notice at her job as home demonstration agent as the wedding date drew near.

Early in the morning on April 7, she walked to her car, parked outside the house where she rented a room. When she opened the door, she saw something poking from under the driver's seat. The open-topped box was small, about six by ten inches, with "tiny pebbles, copper wire, and a flashlight" inside. Her landlord came when she called for help and carried the box to a vacant area while Imogene called the police.

In the box, the Edenton police chief saw picture-frame wire attached to a flashlight battery and blasting powder. As he carried the box into the police station, the crude bomb exploded, burning his arms and legs.

Studying the bomb remnants, SBI agents thought that it was designed more to scare Imogene than to harm her. The agents had worked William Cochrane's case since his gruesome New Year's Eve death three years earlier. They decided to question again the suspect who had remained at the top of their list: George Smith. His name had gone on the suspect list after Cochrane died because George had long been fixated on Imogene. The two grew up together in Pittsboro, their houses only a tenth of a mile from each other. They'd been childhood friends.

In Pittsboro, the Chatham County sheriff knew that George remained a suspect, and he'd kept his eye on him. He later said, "I have driven by

Smith's house at least 10,000 times in the past two years. But, there was never anything note worthy."

The weekend before the bombing, Imogene had traveled to Pittsboro to visit her parents. Perhaps George Smith had seen her somewhere while she was visiting? Or maybe town gossip about her engagement had gotten back to him? Had he secreted the device in her car during that visit? Some thought it unlikely since the three-hour drive back to Edenton could have jostled it enough to make it explode.

The agents questioned George at the service station where he worked. They could tell their questions made him nervous, but he let them vacuum the interior of his car and they took their leave, although they didn't let George out of their sight. They waited down the road and followed him as he left work. He drove straight to his parents' home, where he still lived. They watched as he parked and started walking across a field toward a stand of trees. Surveillance in a rural area is tricky. They lost him in the woods near a quarry and gave up the search when it started raining heavily.

The next morning, George's family became worried. He had disappeared with no word. The local police and the agents joined them in the search and soon found George's body slumped against a tree. He'd shot himself in the chest with his .22 rifle, probably not long after the agents lost sight of him the day before.

Examining what they vacuumed from his car, they found grainy material similar to that found in the bomb box and found a bit of copper wire in his coat pocket. They didn't spend much time on detailed comparisons of the evidence. The thirty-eight-year-old bachelor's suicide was convincing enough.

Over the years, George had often asked Imogene for dates. Although she repeatedly said no, she told him that they'd always be friends. George obviously kept hoping for a different answer.

LONG UNSOLVED

In a region more rural than urban, where families have lived and worked in the same places for decades—or even centuries—crimes can be hard to solve because people in close-knit communities know the wisdom of keeping their mouths shut. Only if someone is willing to talk, even decades later, can cold cases be solved.

The VISTA Murder

What attracts a storyteller to a particular tale? What makes that story burrow under the writer's skin, causing an itch only scratched by digging into what happened and telling others about it? Journalist Mark I. Pinsky said that, for him, such a story was the mysterious death of a young woman in the North Carolina mountains in June 1970. He didn't know Nancy Morgan, but they were about the same age, just starting their lives. Pinsky had recently graduated from Duke University and was headed to the prestigious Columbia School of Journalism and a career as an investigative journalist. That summer, he closely followed the stories of her death and her work in Madison County with Volunteers in Service to America (VISTA), a federal antipoverty program.

The case went cold before the first anniversary of her murder. Years later, a confession brought it back to life. During the intervening time, Pinsky's career took him to Los Angeles and Orlando, and he wrote for the Associated Press, the *Wall Street Journal*, the *New York Times*, *USA Today* and others. He wrote books on both crime and religion and taught courses at Rollins College, North Carolina Central University and the University of Central Florida, among others. But he never forgot the story of Nancy Morgan, even though some might have wished he would.

Nancy had graduated from Southern Illinois University and signed on for the recently created program designed to serve the nation's impoverished people, much as the Peace Corps served abroad. Partnering with Mars Hill College, VISTA sent a team to Madison County, about twenty miles slightly northwest of Asheville—and a world away.

During the Civil War, the county earned the name "Bloody Madison" after thirteen Union sympathizers were killed in a Confederate raid searching out deserters and sympathizers in Shelton Laurel, a settlement of subsistence farmers dating from the 1700s.

One hundred years later, some things hadn't changed. Not everyone welcomed the VISTA volunteers. Mountain folks—like anyone else—can be sensitive to slights or to others thinking that they know better how they ought to live their lives, which adds fuel to an innate suspicion of outsiders in any closed community. Those cultural resentments were close to the surface in 1970.

The VISTA volunteers also challenged other cultural and generational boundaries when they arrived in Madison County. A young woman living and traveling the countryside alone, spending time with unattached male friends, smoking in public—those things just weren't done by proper girls. But could a newly graduated sociology major from up north, fired by a desire to help the underprivileged, possess the receptors to pick up on the subtle signals? Would she be attuned to expectations about behavior so very different from what she'd experienced in college or grown up with at home? Could she understand that what was, to her, innocent behavior might signal something else to those raised within more strictly divided roles for men and women?

By June, Nancy's year with VISTA was in its final weeks. The children she worked with were out of school for the summer, and on June 13, she loaded a group into the county van for a trip to the swimming pool at Mars Hill College. Ed Walker, another VISTA volunteer, also brought a group to the pool that day.

The volunteers lived in rental houses scattered around the county, but they got to know one another and formed friendships as they worked together. At the pool that day, Ed invited Nancy to come over to his cabin

Mars Hill College (now University) partnered with VISTA in 1970 to provide services in surrounding mountain communities. *Photo by Cathy Pickens.*

on Sunday evening, if she didn't have anything better to do. She would soon leave Madison County to start nursing school in New York, and this would be one of their last opportunities for a visit. They were workmates who shared a passion for this new social endeavor. But later, others would read more salacious or sinister motives into that casual Sunday dinner and TV movie.

Nancy rented a hundred-year-old cabin in Shelton Laurel from the Cutshalls, who also owned a small store. Glendora Cutshall said Nancy always brushed aside her concerns, but Glendora worried about her driving around to meetings and such after dark. She cautioned Nancy about coming back from Ed's cabin by herself. The Bluff community was only about ten miles from Shelton Laurel, but on crooked mountain roads, travel must be measured in time, not miles. The trip could take as much as an hour each way. Nancy once again brushed aside Glendora's concerns.

At Ed's, she cooked an omelet and made a salad for their dinner. A couple of other volunteers stopped by after dinner to watch a movie with them, and then the two sat on Ed's porch and talked into the small hours of the morning about what they'd faced working in their two communities, what had been meaningful or felt successful to them and what the odds were that the program would be continued.

Ed said Nancy was excited about nursing school. When her uniform and nursing cap arrived in the mail, she modeled them for some of her friends. After her training, she planned to return to Madison County, with skills that could help people who needed better healthcare.

They had a lot to talk about, and she didn't leave Ed's cabin until about 3:30 a.m. He watched to make sure she got down his steep, narrow driveway to the main road. She should've gotten back to her cabin about 4:30 a.m. that Monday morning.

By Tuesday, the far-flung VISTA team realized that Nancy was missing. The likely explanation was an accident—that her car was down the side of a mountain somewhere between Bluff and Shelton Laurel. They started searching.

On Wednesday morning, a local named Jimmy Lewis pulled onto a logging road off U.S. 70-25, driving east from Hot Springs toward home. When he got out to relieve himself, he didn't expect to see a gray sedan mired in mud—or to find Nancy Morgan's body in the backseat, nude, bound hands to feet with a rope around her neck.

The case became a jurisdictional hot potato. Murders are usually handled by local police—in a city by the police department or in the county by a sheriff. A local agency can call in state police—in North Carolina, the State Bureau of Investigation (SBI)—if special expertise is needed. The FBI has specific jurisdiction over only certain federal crimes, like forgery, or crimes that cross state lines, like kidnapping. Even though Nancy was a federal employee, driving a government-issued vehicle, her murder didn't give the FBI jurisdiction, although the local officials could request assistance.

The FBI helped work the crime scene when Nancy's body was found, but it soon relinquished control to the sheriff and the SBI, whose working theory was that the VISTA outsiders had a wild party with wilder sex and Nancy died. It had to be the outsiders. What reason would someone from Madison County have for killing her?

A LITTLE MORE THAN a year after Nancy's murder, another young woman was found dead, dumped at the side of a road about sixty miles away from Hot Springs. At first, investigators and the public speculated about a connection between Nancy and June Love Barker, a first-year home economics teacher at Sylva-Webster High School. The murders of two young professional women in the region raised concerns. But even though Nancy's death was mentioned in the early news reports of June's murder, the dissimilarities were also clear.

June lived with her parents, who called the sheriff when she didn't return home one Tuesday evening. The sheriff, her parents and others started searching immediately and found her car about midnight on N.C. Highway 107 about sixteen miles outside Sylva.

The next afternoon, a passerby stopped when he spotted what he thought might be blood on the roadside. He found her clothed body rolled down a steep embankment about six miles from where her car was abandoned. The twenty-two-year-old had been killed with a shotgun.

June's murder was solved quickly and put an end to associations with Nancy's murder. A fellow teacher and coach at Sylva's high school, James E. Barnwell, was arrested and eventually convicted for shooting her.

Although Barnwell claimed his actions should be judged as involuntary manslaughter, the facts hinted at a lover's quarrel and more premeditation than the defendant would admit. While engaged to marry June, James Barnwell also dated Maureen Gilligan for a few weeks. He apparently showed June a letter Maureen had written him and told her that they would "discuss it later." The contents of the bloodstained letter, found the day after the shooting, indicated that Maureen had no idea he was already

The trial in June Love Barker's murder was held in Sylva's courthouse. *Photo by Cathy Pickens.*

engaged. Maureen believed she and James were more involved than he admitted to police.

Over defense objections, her letter was admitted into evidence. The jury debated for less than two hours before convicting Barnwell of second-degree murder.

Mark Pinsky put to good use his Duke University political science degree as he explored the roiling waters of Madison County politics in his decades-long investigation of Nancy's case. Former sheriff E.Y. Ponder—known as "the legendary sheriff of Madison County who never carried a gun and always wore a suit"—had won back the job based in part on his claim that he could solve Nancy's murder. Reelected Sheriff Ponder ran a tight political machine, with informants scattered around the county. He focused his investigation on former VISTA worker Ed Walker, the man who'd invited Nancy to a farewell dinner. In 1984, fourteen years after Nancy's murder, Ed was arrested at his home in Florida.

The Old Marshall Jail Hotel, once the domain of Sheriff E.Y. Ponder, sits between the Madison County Courthouse and the French Broad River. *Photo by Cathy Pickens.*

Election stickers for Sheriff Ponder and others are on display in the bar at the Old Marshall Jail Hotel. *Photo by Cathy Pickens.*

One of Sheriff Ponder's many informants, Jimmy Waldroup, told the district attorney a fantastic tale, and he repeated it at Ed's trial. He'd been Ed's neighbor and had seen Nancy through the window at Ed's cabin, naked on the sofa with another man, a rope around her neck. Waldroup went inside the house to help Nancy. Ed Walker ordered him to help dispose of the body or he'd end up dead too. He drove Ed's car to the logging road while Ed drove Nancy's car and ditched it.

Some questioned why the district attorney would bring a prosecution based on such a tale. Joe Huff, the court-appointed defense attorney—and no political fan of Sheriff Ponder's—ripped into Waldroup on cross-examination, emphasizing for the jury that Waldroup's testimony won him favors on a theft conviction. The cross-examination got so heated that Waldroup asked for a bathroom break. The judge said no. Waldroup got up and left the courtroom anyway and was seen from the window heading off down the street.

The jury discussed the case for about an hour and acquitted Ed Walker, but not before he lost his savings, his house and the life he'd built in Florida as a result of his arrest and prosecution.

Nancy's case was still unsolved.

AT THE TIME NANCY disappeared, a group of ten- and eleven-year-old children she worked with told police they'd seen Nancy driving her car on the Tuesday between the time she left Ed's house in the early morning and when her body was found on Wednesday. They insisted it was Nancy—they knew her and her car.

One of them commented as the car drove past, "Look what's in the car with Nancy." Two men sat in the back seat, and a long-haired male rode in the front passenger seat. One boy said he knew it was her "because my uncle won a cake walk with her once and I know her real well."

Perhaps the testimony of kids wasn't taken seriously, especially when it didn't fit the official wild-party-on-the-mountain theory. But the children's account made sense, given other tales about what really happened.

NANCY MORGAN'S CASE DIDN'T disappear, but what circulated were rumors rather than headlines. Mark Pinsky continued his personal investigation during those times when he could get back to the mountains. The stories he heard echoed what the children had said years earlier—about three men seen with her in her government car. The rumors said some local guys from Hot Springs were responsible. One name in particular grabbed Pinsky's interest: Richard Johnson, the son of a Hot Springs police chief, a young man with a nasty reputation and a history of working as one of Sheriff Ponder's team of informants.

In 1998, Johnson gave Pinsky permission to interview him in state prison. Johnson told a story both disturbing and believable, a story that pulled together the rumors about what happened in Hot Springs.

HOT SPRINGS FIRST BECAME a destination in the early 1800s when an entrepreneur from Asheville bought land around the natural mineral spring and built the 350-room Warm Springs Hotel, with a dining room that seated 600 guests. A second massive hotel, the Mountain Park Hotel, was built in 1886. In 1916, the hotel became an internment camp for German sailors captured in U.S. ports at the start of World War I, although "internment" didn't accurately describe their stay. The German prisoners generally enjoyed freedom of movement and the hospitality of Hot Springs, and some remained in the area after the war ended.

Eventually, the two hotels burned or fell into disrepair, construction of the interstate highway bypassed Hot Springs and the springs ceased to be a tourist draw. The small town turned to hosting hikers from the Appalachian Trail, which runs along Main Street and across a bridge over the French Broad River.

Johnson told Pinsky that he and four other men had been hanging out on Sunday afternoon near the bridge when they saw Nancy driving past. She would have taken that route to Ed Walker's cabin. The men were still partying when she drove back by in the wee morning hours of Monday.

They jumped into two cars and followed her, blocking her car and kidnapping her at gunpoint. Johnson detailed how she begged and bargained with them. He said kidnapping and rape weren't new to this crew and that they'd never faced any consequences. But after Nancy disappeared, he said then former sheriff Ponder sent him a message saying that if they had Nancy, they needed to let her go—that a federal volunteer wasn't an ordinary woman.

Johnson said Nancy was killed that Tuesday night, and they drove her and her car to the woods at Tanyard Gap and the logging road where the motorist found her after sunrise.

Johnson, in a later interview with Pinsky and Ed Walker, repeated the story, this time including his own part, the names of the others and details

Left: A gate sits at the entrance of the Hot Springs Resort and Spa near the French Broad River Bridge. *Photo by Cathy Pickens.*

Right: The bridge over the French Broad River is part of the Appalachian Trail through Hot Springs. *Photo by Cathy Pickens.*

of the scene that had never been made public, even at Walker's trial. They knew they were in trouble, he said. He'd told Ponder what happened, more than once, but Ponder "didn't want to believe it."

During the interview, Pinsky asked what Johnson would say to Nancy's brother. He said, "I'm so sorry that it happened. Things just got out of hand. There ain't no good way to put it."

At the time Pinsky interviewed him, Johnson was serving a life sentence for another murder—one more deliberate and, if possible, more diabolical and senseless than Nancy Morgan's murder.

IN JUNE 1984, FOURTEEN years after Nancy died, Johnson still lived in Hot Springs. He and his wife had separated three months earlier, and his eleven-year-old son, Christopher, and five-year-old daughter, Joyce, were living with him.

One early June day, his son was rushed to Mission Memorial Hospital in Asheville with pinpoint pupils, profuse sweating, slurred speech and chest tightness—symptoms of organophosphate insecticide poisoning. Fortunately, the physician diagnosed it quickly, and Christopher responded well to the antidote and left the hospital the next day showing no lingering effects.

About two weeks later, Christopher's little sister, Joyce, was taken to the emergency room in Asheville. She was diagnosed with a urinary tract infection, indicated by pain, nausea and headache. The doctor prescribed an antibiotic and sent her home.

Two days later, Johnson gave Joyce a teaspoonful of white liquid and asked Christopher to look after his sister while he went to eat breakfast at the café in town. Christopher said that soon after his dad left, Joyce started foaming at the mouth. She had trouble walking and talking, and her stomach was growling loud enough for him to hear. She lay on the bed and didn't move. He later said that the liquid his dad spooned into her mouth smelled like bug poison.

An emergency medical technician (EMT) eating breakfast at the same café said Johnson asked him an odd question. He came over to him that morning wanting to know where the ambulance was. It had been moved to the garage for repainting, the EMT said, and asked why he wanted to know.

"I might need it later," Johnson said.

As soon as Johnson got home from his breakfast, he found Joyce ill, grabbed her up and took her to the ambulance garage. On her second visit to Mission Memorial Hospital, the physician found Joyce unresponsive with no pulse; her pupils were pinpoints. To the physician, the foam around her mouth smelled like an organophosphate, such as Malathion or one of several insecticides widely used in homes and on farms—the kind of chemical that would produce the symptoms he observed.

He also knew this reaction wasn't from a long, slow exposure to small amounts of the poison or to absorption through the skin. The little girl must have swallowed the poison between thirty minutes and two hours of the time she started showing symptoms. Joyce's small body did not respond to treatment, and her brain shut down. Life support was removed three days later.

Johnson was tried for Joyce's murder. A friend testified that Johnson had told him that half a teaspoon of the insecticide would kill a person. Dr. Page Hudson, the state's chief medical examiner, testified that the postmortem exam, the analysis of Joyce's stomach contents and the observations by Joyce's brother and the emergency room physician all pointed to Joyce swallowing at least a teaspoon of Diazinon.

Johnson took the witness stand at his trial and testified that he'd sprayed his house for bugs and left the container on the back porch. His father—the former Hot Springs police chief—testified for his son, saying that he took the insecticide container to the hospital himself when the doctor who examined Christopher asked if any of the poison remained.

Johnson denied that he'd asked about the ambulance's location and that he'd told a friend how much insecticide it took to kill someone. He also denied what the prosecution contended was his motive for poisoning his children. He denied saying he "would rather see the kids in hell as his wife have them." He said he loved his children.

The jury found him guilty of first-degree murder.

In his appeal, his attorneys argued that the prosecution failed to prove he had the specific intent to kill Joyce, one of the elements of first-degree murder under North Carolina law. The appellate court acknowledged that, in general, "first-degree murder has been historically defined in this State as the unlawful killing of a human being with malice and with premeditation and deliberation." However, the state's statute defines four categories of first-degree murder. The first category is murder by poison, lying in wait, imprisonment, starving or torture. Then the statute adds three other categories: "any other kind of willful, deliberate and premeditated killing"; murder during the commission of certain other felonies (such as arson, rape, kidnapping or burglary); or felonies committed with a deadly weapon.

The court in this case clearly distinguished these as four distinct categories, emphasizing that willfulness or premeditation need not be proved if poison is used. The poison alone makes the death a first-degree murder.

Richard Johnson's appeal clarified the law for future poisoners. As of 2022, Johnson, age seventy-four, was still incarcerated; by this point, he had posted an astonishing 157 infractions during his time in prison.

The clinical language used in a legal appeal or a medical examiner's testimony can mask the basic truth of what sent Johnson to prison: he tried to kill his little boy and succeeded in killing his little girl because he didn't want his wife to have the children.

Whatever his role in the kidnapping and death of Nancy Morgan, that case remains officially unsolved. In a 2022 update to his book, Mark Pinsky said Johnson had never recanted the confession he made when he and Ed Walker interviewed him in prison.

In the end, the political, social and cultural differences and upheavals in Madison County were only background noise to a shocking act of evil.

The Boone Bathtub Murders

The most intractable puzzles are often those with the most ordinary backdrops. The split-level home of Bryce and Virginia Durham, just off the N.C. 105 Bypass in Boone, was a nice home in a quiet neighborhood, not the kind of place that plays host to unexplained violence.

In 1972, the Durham family had lived in Boone only eighteen months. Bryce had worked for a Mount Airy car loan company before moving to Boone to take over the Buick dealership. His business partner had backed out, but Bryce managed to shoulder the operation with the help of his wife and eighteen-year-old son, Bobby Joe. Things seemed to be going well for the family's new venture.

At about three o'clock on Thursday afternoon, February 3, snow started falling. By nine o'clock that night, about three inches blanketed the ground, and snow was still falling.

Folks who live in the mountains know how to navigate snowy roads. Bryce didn't hesitate to drive to his evening Rotary meeting—a special meeting held not at its usual location at the Holiday Inn but at Appalachian Ski Mountain, about halfway between Boone and Blowing Rock. A group of Green Berets was conducting ski training at the resort and giving a demonstration for the Rotary Club that evening.

When the meeting broke up after eight o'clock, the club members all headed back toward Boone. Bryce stopped by the dealership about 8:30 p.m. and asked one of the staff to gas up the new green-and-white Jimmy, a four-wheel-drive that had just been delivered. He wanted to make sure he could make it up the steep road to his house as the snow got deeper.

His wife, Virginia, had stayed in the office working on some tax documents that evening. Their son Bobby had driven over from Appalachian State sometime after the snow started to ride home with his parents.

The Durhams' daughter, Jenny, and her husband, Troy Hall, lived only a few miles from her parents. That evening, the couple started watching the Winter Olympics from Sapporo, Japan, but the TV picture died, so they put a record on the stereo player. Their phone rang, and Jenny heard her husband ask, "Virginia, is that you?"

Troy returned to the TV room and asked Jenny if her mother would play a prank. He said that when he answered the phone, Virginia whispered, asking for help and saying that three men were beating Bryce and Bobby in the back of the house. Then the phone went dead.

When Jenny called her parents' phone and got only a busy signal, she and Troy grabbed their coats and headed out into the snowstorm. Questions would later arise about whether Virginia had really called. At the time, the technology couldn't track pings from cellphone towers or identify phones operating in a radius around a crime scene. In 1971, local calls weren't even noted in the phone company's records.

Troy had just come home from studying at the campus library not long before the phone call, but now his car wouldn't start. The couple went to the home of their trailer park manager, Cecil Small, and asked him for a lift to the Durhams' house. Small also happened to work as a private detective.

Navigating the four miles of snowy roads took about twenty minutes. The hill up to the house looked treacherous, so Jenny stayed in the car at the bottom of the hill. The two men walked up the driveway and around the house, checking things out, and found the garage door partially open. The door into the house from the garage was unlocked.

Inside, they made their way from the den to the kitchen. Someone had torn the phone from the wall—which had to have happened soon after

Busy King Street in Boone is backed by mountains. *Courtesy of Jeremy Mikkola via Creative Commons and marked with CC BY 2.0.*

Virginia talked to her son-in-law. Then the men heard a noise somewhere in the house—or thought they did. They couldn't use the phone to call for help, so they rejoined Jenny at the car and tried to drive to a nearby house, but the car got stuck. Eventually, they found a phone and called the authorities.

When investigators arrived on scene, they entered through the front door rather than the garage. From that entry point, the open bathroom door was visible as soon as they took a few steps inside the front entrance.

The crime scene was bizarre. Virginia, Bryce and Bobby had apparently gotten home and started eating a snack in front of the TV before someone interrupted them. All three had their hands bound behind their backs and were bent over with their heads submerged in the bathtub. Their faces were bruised, and the water in the tub was running, flooding the floor.

Bobby's body was near the faucet, apparently the first submerged in the water. Bryce was beside him, and Virginia was on the end of the tub. Bryce had a thin rope loosely looped around his throat. Virginia had been strangled to death, and she appeared to have been the last one placed in the water. The father and son had both been strangled by a rope but ultimately died from drowning in the bathwater.

As a gauge of what the family had encountered when they came home, investigators looked at their shoes. Virginia's and Bobby's shoes were lined up near the front door, as if they had a habit of removing them when they got home. Bryce's pull-on waterproof shoe coverings were upstairs in the bedroom, along with his overcoat. He still wore his lace-up dress shoes, so he'd come upstairs but hadn't yet removed his shoes.

Whatever happened to them occurred after they got home and began to settle in for the evening. None of the three adults was frail, and one of them was an athletic eighteen-year-old. More than one attacker had to be present to subdue and kill all three. Strangulation and drowning are slow methods of death, so none of this happened quickly. The local investigators had never dealt with anything like what they found in this house. The Watauga County Sheriff's Office called in the State Bureau of Investigation (SBI).

The only blood on the scene was a small amount on the carpet from Virginia's bloody nose. No suspect hairs or fibers were identified, so no DNA from the perpetrators was available, even had they been able to test that in 1972. Investigators considered possible links to a team of house burglars operating in the area but found no connection. For one thing, the car dealership's night bank deposit sat in a bag on the dining room table, untouched.

Police found a witness who saw the GMC truck Bryce had driven home that night turning onto Highway 105 toward Boone as the witness turned toward Linville. He took note of the truck because the driver almost ran him off the road.

When the witness returned home at about 10:30 p.m., he again saw the Jimmy, abandoned in a ditch about two miles from the Durhams' house, the engine still running, with the lights and windshield wipers on. Some decorative silver items stolen from the house were left in the back seat.

Over the next forty years, authorities interviewed more than two hundred people. They investigated the son-in-law and others close to the family. Early on, they arrested four men but quickly cleared them. They asked whether son Bobby could have been involved with drugs on the Appalachian State campus or whether Bryce's dealings in Mount Airy had been shady or dangerous. Was this a professional hit? An emotionless murder done for money? Or for revenge? Could they find any other crime that fit this triple homicide pattern? They found nothing that answered their questions.

As in any thorough investigation, authorities came back to the case whenever an advance in technology offered hope of new information from old evidence. The technology for searching fingerprint databases for matches has continued to improve, so they've scanned fingerprints through the increasingly sophisticated systems. As DNA technology developed and continued to improve, they had the physical evidence tested for DNA. They found no matches to any physical evidence.

They also followed up on rumors that Bryce had snitched on a dealership odometer-rollback scam in Surry County. No evidence of that. Also no evidence, despite the apparent "military precision" of the attack on the Durhams, that the Green Beret demonstration at the ski resort had any connection. Was it a random home invasion? Or perhaps a disgruntled customer or supplier? Some sort of retaliation or personal vendetta? No matter how far-fetched, they explored the options and found no evidence for any of that.

More than one person had to be involved to subdue and kill three adults. Ligature strangulation and drowning are intimate, up-close murders, and they take time. Someone was determined to finish what they'd started.

Interviewed thirty-five years after the murders, retired investigator Charles Whitman said they consulted an FBI profiler early in the case. "He told us the longer the perpetrator can go without confessing to anybody, the easier it becomes" to pretend someone else did it, that you weren't involved. These killers have had plenty of time to convince themselves of a different script for what happened and why.

Some of the initial investigators retired or moved to other jobs, and some died. The case even got the attention of a homegrown and influential politician. Rufus Edmisten may be best known for his work on U.S. Senator Sam Ervin's staff during the Watergate hearings, but for those in Watauga County in 1974, they remember his election as the state's attorney general and how he made sure the case had the attention of state investigators. That attention meant a lot to the people in town. Even if the locals didn't know the Durhams personally, their murders hit too close to home.

Investigators outside the state also got involved. The Durham family murders became the very first case discussed by the Vidocq Society in Philadelphia, a gathering of expert crime solvers named for an eighteenth-century French criminal who became one of the world's first criminalists.

In 1990, three friends formed the Vidocq Society: William Fleisher, police officer turned FBI agent turned U.S. Customs agent; forensic sculptor Frank Bender; and prison psychologist Richard Walter. The by-invitation-only group draws its eighty-two members—for the eighty-two years Vidocq lived—from law enforcement and forensic science professionals. Law enforcement agencies wrestling with difficult cold case homicides apply to present their cases at the group's monthly lunch meeting, hoping to get new leads or new directions from the collected expertise.

For psychologist Richard Walter, the Vidocq Society was a continuation of the interests that consumed his life. Michael Capuzzo, who wrote about the society and its cases, summarized Walter's philosophy: "Each man had a purpose in life, Walter believed; his was to identify, torment, and defeat the most depraved psychopaths on Earth. To be good at it, to be one of the five best in the world, he had rid himself of distractions, had married his profession. Destroying evil gave him the greatest pleasure."

One Vidocq member saw in the Durham family tragedy similarities with the Cutter family murders in Kansas, recounted in Truman Capote's classic *In Cold Blood*. The case didn't seem like light luncheon entertainment.

Walter said that murder wasn't entertaining—except for the murderer. In introducing the case to the group, he said, "One can discern from this crime scene that for this kind of personality, it's the satisfaction of a mission accomplished, a job well done. Oftentimes, the uninitiated fail to grasp how much pleasure is involved for the killer."

Before the September meeting in 1990, North Carolina's SBI had hired Walter to look at the case, which he found "a wonderful case." By then, the murders were eighteen years old. After reviewing the fact summary and photos, the Vidocq members started questioning Walter. Was it a robbery? "No, on the contrary, it was rather clumsily staged to look like a robbery. But it was a killing all about power and control."

Was it a grudge killing? The sheriff had found no one with enough anger toward anyone in the family to prompt the killings. And though arrests were made in a burglary ring case, no one was prosecuted for the murders.

Members asked Walter about the Durhams' son-in-law. His marriage with their daughter was in trouble, and the couple later divorced, so Walter found that interesting.

What about Cecil Small, the private investigator who managed the trailer park? Walter said, "There's reason to question his general credibility." Small insisted that he'd personally witnessed a Cuban or Mexican man run from the area carrying a rifle immediately after President John F. Kennedy was shot. He had credibility issues but no viable link to the Durham crime.

So, who killed the Durham family? Walter cryptically replied that he had a theory. "We'll see if the state police are savvy enough to go forward with it." Apparently the theory didn't pan out or the evidence couldn't be gathered to support charges, because the case remained unsolved. Despite all the theories and the long investigation, could it, in the end, be as random and senseless as the 1959 murders of the Cutter family in Holcomb, Kansas?

THE FIFTIETH ANNIVERSARY OF the murders passed on February 3, 2022. Six days later, Watauga County sheriff Len Hagaman held a bombshell news conference. He named the four men who, according to evidence, killed the Durham family: Billy Sunday Birt, Bobby Gene Gaddis, Billy Wayne Davis and Charles David Reed.

Most who'd followed the case were surprised to learn that the killers were members of the Dixie Mafia. The FBI described the Dixie Mafia as "a loose confederation of thugs and crooks" operating primarily in Georgia, Alabama, Mississippi and Texas. The North Georgia branch started running illegal liquor in the 1960s. In 1967, they rigged ten sticks of dynamite to North Georgia district attorney Floyd Hoard's car and killed him instantly. What had started as an illegal liquor-running operation blossomed into a ruthless, far-reaching criminal enterprise. Violent armed robbery, auto theft, bank robberies, burglary and drug dealing topped the list of activities, and dynamite remained a favorite method for sending messages and eliminating threats. Billy Sunday Birt admitted to committing fifty-six murders in his career.

The four men had been convicted in the 1973 torture-murders of the Flemings, a couple in their seventies who owned a Georgia used car lot. The gang heard that the Flemings kept as much as $40,000 at their house, but they found only $4,000 in coins stored in canning jars in an outbuilding. As with the Durhams, they strangled the couple, but this time they omitted the bathtub.

The break in the Durham case came when Birt's son Shane visited the White County Sheriff's Office in Georgia, just south of Murphy and Franklin, North Carolina. Shane was helping with research on a book about Georgia crime cases. He mentioned a story his dad had told him about three murders they'd done in Boone and how they'd almost gotten stuck in a snowstorm that night.

When the Georgia sheriff called with that bit of information, Sheriff Hagaman took the tip seriously. Hagaman had been a Boone police officer and involved in the Durham case since soon after the murders.

In September 2019, the North Carolina investigators traveled to Georgia's Augusta State Medical Prison for the first of three separate interviews, spread over two years, with eighty-one-year-old Billy Wayne Davis. Davis was the only surviving member of the gang who drove up the steep driveway to the Durham house that night. He was serving a life sentence, and the other three men had died in prison, convicted of murders eerily similar to the Durham family's.

Investigators corroborated Davis's statements with other witnesses and with the crime scene evidence. At the 2022 press conference, Hagaman said, "We are confident that we now know who committed these crimes."

Davis told Watauga investigators that the men were hired to do a hit at that house. He either doesn't know or won't say who ordered the hit. As Vidocq Society psychologist Richard Walter surmised, the murders were about power and control.

From the beginning, some of the leads that investigators followed in the 1970s headed in the right direction, although they didn't result in any arrests at the time. They suspected a connection with Bryce Durham's work in auto financing or his car dealership, and Fleming coincidentally ran a used car lot. But investigators haven't commented whether any connection actually existed.

Others still speculate about son-in-law Troy Hall's involvement. Hagaman said he would like to interview Hall again, but he died in 2019. Hagaman added, "Unfortunately, whoever arranged the murders is forever lost due to the death of Billy Sunday Birt," who died in 2017.

The other two men at the Durhams' house have also died. When interviewed in 2022, Davis was in a medical prison unit, reportedly suffering from dementia. He admitted that he was in Boone that night. He said he drove the getaway car, although in an online post, someone who knew Davis said that his history suggests he would have been more involved than the role of getaway driver implies. If Davis remembers anything else about the case, he's keeping it to himself.

MURDER IN CHINA

Appalachian State University attracts students from around the world, particularly those who love snow skiing, hiking and other outdoor activities. But like many universities, App State, as it is called, also offers opportunities to leave the Boone campus to study abroad. Even as the students and faculty live in an unaccustomed culture and learn to navigate the unknown and unexpected, they remain very much a part of the campus, connected with their friends and colleagues back in Boone.

In 1987, Appalachian offered a robust study-abroad program, enlisting faculty and students for the international trips. Dr. Allen Kindt became a visiting professor of piano at China's Shenyang Conservatory of Music. His wife, Mary Jo "Jody" Kindt, and stepdaughter, eighteen-year-old Erin Johnston, accompanied him. Erin was taking a gap year before starting as a freshman at the University of North Carolina–Chapel Hill. She and her mother were teaching in Shenyang, a major industrial city closer to the North Korean border than to Beijing. The family lived in a walled apartment complex with other visiting foreign students and faculty.

Erin considered teaching English as a second language (ESL) courses to Chinese students as good preparation. She planned to teach high school English after she finished college. Erin was outgoing and determined to get the most out of her adventure in China. She'd made many friends among the other visiting foreigners, in particular students from North Korea, a Tanzanian medical student she dated, a Canadian professor and a few Chinese soccer players.

On January 23, 1988, Erin's mother came upstairs in their apartment to let her know she had a phone call. Jody was stunned to find her daughter in bed, dead from what was described as a "sharp object that penetrated approximately 3 inches into her brain."

As news of the tragedy spread within the academic enclave, most of the other Appalachian students decided to return home. One of Erin's close friends, Lora Lynn Hodges, remained for a few weeks before coming back to the States. In a news interview, Hodges said she had harbored doubts about the level of security in the student apartment complex. One day Erin had found maintenance workers sitting on her bed, looking through her photo album, when they were supposed to be doing repairs in the Kindts' apartment. The maintenance staff had keys and easy access everywhere in the complex.

The Chinese authorities investigated suspects in addition to the maintenance staff. Goa Shu, a professional Chinese soccer player who knew Erin, was arrested for a period and then released. They also scrutinized the medical student she dated, suspicious about their relationship because Erin also had a boyfriend back in Boone. Erin and the medical student had quarreled the night before her death because he was spending too much time with other friends. Erin's friend Lora Lynn "couldn't even fathom" that he could have been involved—he was too calm. But in China, couples don't start dating until after they finish their education, and then it is for the purpose of marriage, not for casual companionship, so Erin's relationships were of intense interest to investigators.

The Canadian professor and Erin had argued at dinner about life in the southern United States. The phone call Erin received the morning her mother discovered her body was the professor, calling to apologize. The authorities seized his passport and detained him for questioning for a day.

Authorities also considered robbery as a motive. Cash had been stolen during a break-in at the Kindts' apartment a few months earlier. Erin's attacker had also taken cash, some inexpensive jewelry and a cassette player from her room.

Lora Lynn and others believed that the killer had to be among the foreign contingent or the workers inside the complex. Those who lived in the compound had little contact with native Chinese citizens outside of classes.

Before Erin's murder, those who planned study-abroad or student-faculty exchange programs with China felt confident about the safety of the participants. China was regarded as one of the safest destinations in the world. Since international relations normalized in the late 1970s, only one other U.S. visitor, a Chinese American from Texas, had been murdered in China, stabbed in a robbery on a train only a few months before Erin's death. The two robbers in that incident were executed in 1987, about the time Erin and her parents arrived in Shenyang. Erin's death prompted universities sending students to programs in China to reevaluate that perception of safety.

On the Chinese side, officials worked to solve the case—they wanted to maintain China's visitor-friendly reputation. News reports indicated that murders during robberies had increased in China in the mid-1980s, but its per capita crime rate continued to be low compared to other countries.

The case remained unsolved, and students from American universities continued to enroll in programs to teach English or study in China—though, for a time, with a dose of caution and concern.

UNSOLVED MOUNTAINTOP MURDER

One of the frustrations of looking at cases gone cold for decades is the realization that perhaps, just perhaps, forensic technology might have solved the case, in a later time or in a different place.

In 1937, when Elva Brannock disappeared on her way to the Dividing Ridge community school in Allegheny County, the list of suspects was surprisingly long for such a sparsely populated place. But crime-solving science wasn't available—just old-fashioned question-the-witnesses detective work. And that didn't prove to be enough.

Elva, at sixteen, was a good-humored, responsible daughter, the youngest of the Brannocks' eight children. On that wintery February morning, she bundled up and gathered her books and lunch pail for the walk to school. She never arrived.

This was the height of the Depression, although in a farming community, people tended to be able to make do, raising their own food and maybe growing tobacco as a cash crop. The area was also a center for what was called the Parkway Project, building the Blue Ridge Parkway, one of the federal initiatives in Roosevelt's Civil Conservation Corps and public works plan.

News took a while to travel, so it wasn't until late that afternoon, when Elva didn't return home, that the family learned she'd never arrived at school. Sheriff Walter Irwin coordinated a team of two hundred searchers, but it took four days to find her body, even though it was resting not far

Sign marking the entrance to the Blue Ridge Parkway. *Photo by Cathy Pickens.*

from the shortcut she and other students took through the woods to the Dividing Ridge School. She was fully clothed with her books beside her, but she had been strangled, and as one report noted, her head and mouth were bruised and beaten. The undisturbed area around her body suggested that she'd been brought to the place and tidied up, as if whoever had done the unspeakable had felt remorse or had known her and cared about her.

Left: Old Saddle Mountain Baptist Church, founded in 1895, was a gathering place for members of the Dividing Ridge community. *Photo by Cathy Pickens.*

Right: Elva Brannock was buried at the cemetery beside Saddle Mountain Church. *Photo by Cathy Pickens.*

That morning, Elva had spoken to a few of the parkway workers as she passed; they, of course, became suspects. A hunter in the area with blood on his clothes also went on the suspect list. Even though the recently formed FBI lab in Washington said that the blood was not animal blood, they had no confession or other evidence to connect the man to her death.

Others pointed to a group of moonshiners operating in the area. Contrary to the hillbilly stereotype, most living in the mountain regions were church-going Baptists who didn't condone drinking or "cooking" illegal whiskey. While the story provided good fodder for newspapers, even the locals who didn't imbibe didn't believe that some crazed band of moonshiners attacked and killed a schoolgirl. Authorities did bust at least four stills in the area, discovered as they searched for Elva and her killer—one still was only two hundred yards from where her body was found. They also questioned a jail escapee who had been arrested for drunk driving in Galax, Virginia. As years passed, they continued to question people, including a man who killed his wife in 1959. No one was ever arrested. No solid leads developed from the interviews. No physical evidence pointed to the killer.

In the 1930s, the locals weren't universally in favor of the CCC work or the outsiders coming into the mountain regions, so naturally some suspicions fell that direction, whether deserved or not. But decades later, the detailed stonework bridges and drainage systems still stand, and in 2020, the scenic highway along the ridges of the Appalachian Mountain chain wound through the most visited national park in the nation. The two-lane parkway runs past where Elva Brannock died on her way to school and where she was buried at her family church.

COLD CASE SOLVED

When an unsolved case lingers for forty years before investigators find the solution, the news must offer some reassurance for those cases that still don't have answers.

On August 26, 1980, Ronda Blaylock's parents reported her missing from her home in Rural Hall. Ronda was just days into her ninth-grade year at Atkins High School, her first year attending a public school.

Ronda's parents both worked. As an only child, the fourteen-year-old spent a few hours every day after school at home on her own. She tended to respect her parents' rule that she stay close to the house while they were at work. On that Tuesday, though, as she walked home past the bowling alley with her friend, a man offered them a ride home in his blue pickup truck. He introduced himself as Jimmy but said his friends called him Butch.

The driver dropped Ronda's friend off at her house first. Ronda never made it home.

According to an alert posted by the Forsyth County Sheriff's Department, Ronda's friend described the truck as immaculately clean, dark blue with a light-blue interior, with an automatic transmission, a CB radio attached under the dash and a low, white camper top with two bubble windows mounted on the back. She described Jimmy as being in his early twenties, just under six feet tall and slender with brownish-blond straight hair cut to feather back on the sides; he had a thin mustache, mirrored aviator sunglasses, a black Budweiser T-shirt, a two-toned baseball cap and hairy arms and smoked Winston cigarettes. Despite the details in her description, neither the man nor the truck could be found.

Ronda's family and friends searched for her for three days. On Friday, less than twenty miles from her home, a body was discovered in the woods off Sechrist Loop Road just north of Pilot Mountain. Authorities collected

"Jimmy" or "Butch"

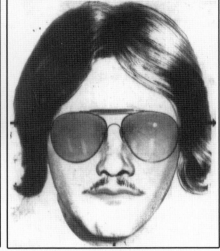

Contact the Ronda Blaylock Task Force at:

Authorities circulated composite sketches of the man witnesses last saw with Ronda Blaylock. *Photo released by "Ronda Blaylock Homicide Task Force" Facebook page.*

dental records for teenage girls missing in Forsyth, Stokes and Surry Counties. The office of the state medical examiner in Chapel Hill used the records to identify Ronda. She had been sexually assaulted and stabbed multiple times.

The Surry County Sheriff's Office interviewed witnesses who'd seen the girls get in the truck near the bowling alley on Tuesday afternoon. They followed up leads on the blue 1970s Chevrolet truck and on men named Jimmy or Butch. By 1982, investigators had run out of leads and the case went cold, but subsequent sheriffs reopened or reexamined the evidence in 2003, 2010 and 2013.

In 2015, the State Bureau of Investigation formed a multi-jurisdictional task force. As part of that effort, investigators created the "Ronda Blaylock Homicide Task Force" Facebook page, posting the details of her abduction with descriptions and sketches of Jimmy and photos of a similar truck. The task force brought together investigators from surrounding counties, the North Carolina State Crime Lab and the South Carolina Law Enforcement Division. In the past, leads had taken investigators to Myrtle Beach, Ohio and Pennsylvania for interviews, with no solid results.

A 1925 postcard describes Pilot Mountain: "In years gone by used by Indians as a guide or pilot." *Courtesy of the Durwood Barbour Collection of North Carolina Postcards, UNC.*

Finally, in August 2020, forty years after Ronda's murder and one year to the day after her mother's death, sixty-four-year-old Robert James Adkins was arrested and charged with first-degree murder and first-degree forcible rape. Adkins's booking photos show a slender-faced man with long gray hair and a scraggly beard. Adkins had been questioned several times in the past, particularly in 2017, but deputies said that he was surprised when they came to arrest him. He had a few alcohol-related driving offenses with suspended sentences but no felony convictions. For almost thirty years, he had lived with his wife in Dobson, in Surry County, about twenty miles from Pilot Mountain and thirty-five miles from Rural Hall. The couple had one son.

The arrest resulted from the collective efforts of the task force and retired officers who combed through the files, re-interviewed witnesses in Myrtle Beach and Ohio and reviewed old reports and forensic evidence that eventually pointed to Adkins.

In December 2020, Adkins, who was in poor health, pleaded guilty to second-degree rape and murder and was sentenced to twenty-one to twenty-five years.

MISSING

In a region with thousands of acres of farmland and wilderness, people can go missing in ways unfathomable in urban settings. Crimes can go unsolved because exposure to the elements hides or destroys evidence.

The Great Smoky Mountains National Park covers 500,000 acres on the North Carolina/Tennessee border and is the most visited of the national parks, hosting more visitors every year than the next three most popular parks (Yosemite, Zion and Rocky Mountain) combined. With 12 million visitors each year, many of them not accustomed to just how wild a wilderness area can be, accidents can happen. No one expects to visit the park and have a friend or loved one simply disappear and never be found...but it happens.

DENNIS MARTIN

Over the last fifty years, those lost in the Appalachian Mountains have benefited from what searchers learned after Dennis Martin disappeared.

In June 1969, grandfather Clyde Martin, dad Bill Martin and his two sons, nine-year-old Doug and six-year-old Dennis, headed to Cades Cove to start their traditional Father's Day weekend camping and hiking trip. After the Knoxville family's first night camping, they hiked to Spence Field just over the North Carolina border from Tennessee. There they met another family from Alabama, also named Martin, and Doug and Dennis joined their two boys in playing. Late afternoon, the adults could see that the boys were concocting some kind of plan on the trail ahead of them, but the parents pretended to be startled when the kids jumped out of the woods to scare them—all the kids except Dennis.

Dennis, the youngest of the four, was dressed in a red shirt, which was too easy to spot among the trees, so the others told him to come from the other side of the trail so he wouldn't spoil the surprise. Only three minutes had passed since Dennis's father saw him running up the Appalachian Trail at his usual quick pace, but he didn't jump out with the others and they couldn't find him.

This was Dennis's first time on this family camping trip, but he and his family were experienced in the woods. Spence Field is a high point subject to stiff and constant winds and surrounded by almost impenetrable rhododendron thickets, known as "laurel hells" to the locals. With the noise and the sameness of the landscape, even an adult can lose his bearings.

At 8:30 p.m. that evening, about five hours after they last saw Dennis, his grandfather Clyde arrived at Cades Cove to notify the rangers. He then

Distinctive blossoms and thick growth of a mountain laurel "hell" in the Great Smoky Mountains National Park. *Courtesy of pfly via flickr.com.*

hiked the six miles back to Spence Field to search along other trails. In mid-June, sunset comes close to nine o'clock, and some light usually remains in the sky for almost another hour. However, that night brought over two inches of heavy rain with thunder, lightning and wind that deepened the chill as the temperature fell to fifty degrees. Dennis was wearing a T-shirt, shorts, socks and lace-up black Oxford shoes—not all-weather gear for a cold, wet night.

Hypothermia was a serious concern: Dennis was small and slender and more susceptible to the damp and cold. A small body loses heat quickly, and hypothermia leads to confusion, an overwhelming sense of sleepiness and a paradoxical sense of warmth. In cold weather, it is not unusual for searchers to find a discarded coat or gloves as a wandering victim begins to feel too warm before lying down to sleep—never to wake up.

At daybreak on Saturday, rangers and experienced hikers searched along the rain-slick trails. That week, as many as 1,400 people joined the search every day, including a Special Forces unit from Fort Bragg in Eastern North Carolina, on site for a training exercise. The weather did not cooperate. Continuing rain prompted flash flooding, prevented search planes from flying and washed away signs of Dennis's movements.

At his family's request, the FBI was called in, and the family offered a $5,000 reward, just on the off chance that Dennis had been kidnapped. Famous psychic Jeane Dixon called with a detailed prediction about where he'd wandered and could be found; the searchers checked that area once again, with no results.

Had he fallen off a precipice or steep mountainside? Had he become disoriented and wandered too far in the wrong direction? Had he encountered a wild boar intent on defending her young? Had he been snatched by a human predator and carried away from the area? The possibilities haunted the family and the searchers.

RETIRED PARK RANGER AND expert tracker Dwight McCarter spoke years later to WBIR TV News about the mistakes made in that search. The search protocol at the time, he said, was the same they used to fight forest fires: "You surrounded it and drowned it." McCarter knew how easy it was to become disoriented in the constant wind on Spence Field and how difficult it would have been for Dennis or his searchers to hear or be heard.

In analyzing the key mistakes in the search, McCarter didn't put much stock in the phone report from a man who said he'd heard a scream the day Dennis disappeared. For one, the distance to the location was too far for

View at Newfound Gap. *Courtesy of Jim R. Rogers via flickr.com and licensed under CC BY-ND 2.0.*

Dennis to have covered in that amount of time. And the tip wasn't called in until a month after the disappearance.

For McCarter, the more important clue was shoeprints found on the mountainside four days into the search—a set of tracks made by a small child's smooth-soled Oxford shoe. At the time, the prints were ignored because a group of Boy Scouts was camping in a shelter nearby. On the fiftieth anniversary of Dennis's disappearance, McCarter told reporter Matt Lakins that those prints could have been important: "They didn't find tracks from a bunch of kids. They found tracks from one kid."

For those with a loved one missing, hundreds of people combing the mountains must be reassuring. But one of the lessons learned in Dennis's case was that smaller, more experienced search teams were less likely to trample or ignore vital evidence. In the next few decades, academic researchers and field specialists in SAR (search and rescue) would begin building databases and predictive models of how a small child or an elderly man with dementia or an experienced hiker might behave in various terrains and where they would most likely go if lost. When Dennis ran up the trail, none of that research had yet been done, but his disappearance spurred people to begin developing better systems.

NATURAL CHANGES OCCUR IN a wilderness area as fifty years pass. Tall trees now shade fields where the search helicopters landed, and the established tree canopy is thicker. The heat, humidity and rainfall in the Smoky Mountains yields a thick undergrowth. Searchers can walk within inches of what they are looking for and never see it. As expert tracker McCarter pointed out, leaf debris falls and decays. "An inch every year builds up on top of the area," he said. Fifty inches have accumulated since Dennis ran up that trail.

The wilderness is wild. Even with the latest technology and techniques, Dennis might still have stayed missing.

TRENNY GIBSON

The Smoky Mountains National Park contains one of the most biodiverse environments in the world. In October 1976, a high school biology class from Knoxville came to the park to study plant life. The bus dropped the students off at the Clingmans Dome parking area at 12:30 p.m. so they could walk to Andrews Bald. They would investigate on their own but weren't to stray from the grassy, open area of the bald. And they were to be back at the bus by 3:30 for the drive home, so they needed to allow time for the almost four-mile roundtrip hike back to the parking area.

View eastward from Clingmans Dome. *Courtesy of Acroterion via Wikimedia Commons and licensed under CC BY-ND 2.0.*

The day was overcast and began misting rain. Sixteen-year-old Trenny Lynn Gibson wore only a blouse and skirt that day, so she borrowed a plaid jacket from a classmate to keep her warm. The students broke into groups and then formed into new groups as they walked along, eating lunch and stopping to take note of certain plants, some students moving faster or slower than others.

Trenny and the rest began following the well-marked trail back to the parking lot at about 2:00 p.m. She moved ahead of one group, and a student saw her turn right into the woods up ahead. No one mentioned it, assuming that she was taking a bathroom break. But when they gathered at the bus for the headcount, Trenny was missing.

The teacher, Mr. Dunlap, sent boys back up the trail and along a branch of the Appalachian Trail to see if they could find her. By citizens band radio, he alerted park authorities at 4:06 p.m. No one called Trenny's parents in Knoxville until the bus got back to the high school at about 8:00 p.m.

Mr. Gibson was flying home that evening from a business trip, so Trenny's parents didn't get to Clingmans Dome until late at night. As requested, they brought some clothes Trenny had worn for the tracking dogs. Heavy rain and dropping temperatures made finding the girl more urgent.

Trackers start with the Point Last Seen (PLS), which would have been where Trenny's classmate saw her step off the trail. They also looked for anything that would indicate a different Last Known Position (LKP)—a footprint, a piece of clothing or a discarded item that could help pinpoint how fast she was moving and in what direction. The only items found where she was last seen were a beer can and three cigarette butts.

During the days of searching, dogs tracked Trenny's scent along the road toward Newfound Gap, and they noted a pile of the same brand of cigarette butts found beside the trail at the spot on the road where her scent disappeared. In the days long before DNA analysis, a popular cigarette brand didn't lead anywhere. And scent dogs aren't infallible.

The searchers considered three options: Trenny wandered off the trail, got disoriented and couldn't find her way back; she arranged a meeting and left the area with someone; or she was kidnapped. That she would have disappeared voluntarily seemed unlikely to her parents. The other two options were terrifying, but the possibility that she'd been abducted from federal land gave the FBI jurisdiction. Agents investigated an overzealous boyfriend back home and other leads, but nothing materialized.

Despite three hundred ground searchers, helicopters from the Tennessee Air National Guard, the FBI and local law enforcement, a second search

Sign marking Newfound Gap at the border of North Carolina and Tennessee. *Courtesy of Jim R. Rogers via flickr.com and licensed under CC BY-ND 2.0.*

conducted the following spring, a psychic and at least one person who called to report seeing Trenny in a dream, no one found any sign of Trenny or any clear evidence of why or how she disappeared. She remains on the list of the national park's unsolved disappearances.

POLLY MELTON

When someone disappears in the dense forests of the Appalachian Mountains, one avenue usually explored is whether the person meant to disappear. Some wondered if Trenny Gibson had run off with someone, although few took that seriously. The same question came up five years later when fifty-eight-year-old Polly Melton walked down a path and vanished.

Polly was married to her third husband, Robert Melton, twenty years her senior. He had two sons, but she had no children. The couple had taken up the life of nomads, living and traveling in their Airstream trailer. In a campground in the Smoky Mountains' Deep Creek area, they had gotten acquainted with other couples who habitually settled there for a few months every summer, and the Meltons joined them again in the summer of 1981.

On September 25, the fall leaves were beginning to color. That afternoon, Polly and two female friends were taking a four-mile hike on the Deep Creek Trail before supper. Polly had been walking this trail for twenty years, and the friends regularly took this route because it wasn't too demanding. Polly, a two-pack-a-day smoker with high blood pressure, wanted to exercise but couldn't do anything too strenuous.

On the return segment of their walking loop, Polly surprised her friends by picking up her pace. Almost as if she was kidding with them, she disappeared over a rise in the trail. Her friends said they thought they would find her breathing heavy and sitting on the bench up ahead. But she wasn't at the bench, so they continued to the campground, thinking she had some reason to hurry back. They didn't find her at her trailer or in the campground either.

Other campers helped search along the short paths that led from the trail to the creek but found nothing. She couldn't have become disoriented and followed another trail because none crossed in that short section between where she'd left her friends and the campground.

The Charley Project maintains a website of more than fifteen thousand cold-case missing person reports. According to Polly's Charley Project report, she was wearing a sleeveless top with pink and white stripes and tan pants. Her crepe-soled shoes had a crack running across the ball of the foot on the left shoe—a distinctive mark that would have been identifiable had any footprints been found. She had her Virginia Slims cigarettes with her but no car keys; because of her medical condition, she had recently stopped driving. She was almost six feet tall, and her photo shows short, curly hair framing a smiling face and large glasses.

By 6:00 p.m., they had notified the park ranger at Deep Creek that Polly was missing.

Much of their usual walk took them along an old gravel road that wasn't part of the park and was still used by vehicles, so following her progress on the packed road was almost impossible. Tracking dogs were brought in the next day, but conditions weren't good for finding a scent trail, and trackers saw no broken branches or signs of passage leaving the road.

Rangers closed that section of the road and trail to visitors for several days, and searchers combed the area on either side and along Deep Creek but found no hint of where she'd gone. The deep pools in the creek were also investigated, in case she had drowned, but they found no sign of her in the water either. Deep Creek is popular for fishing and tube-floating, but over the years, no one has found anything related to Polly's disappearance.

The Deep Creek trailhead, where Polly Melton took regular walks with her friends. *Photo by Cathy Pickens.*

As with any missing person, when the immediate scene fails to yield clues, investigators started digging into the background of Polly and her family. Her mother had died a few years earlier and Polly missed her deeply, but she was still close with her father. In the past, she had taken medication for depression; her husband's Valium was missing, but no one noticed her

Deep Creek near the start of the trail. *Photo by Cathy Pickens.*

carrying any medication or cash with her on her walk. They found only one variation in her normal routine: she didn't go to serve meals that day at the Bryson City Presbyterian Church Nutrition Center.

The inevitable speculation arose. Had she left willingly? Had someone picked her up, and she left her life with Robert behind? Had she been abducted? The FBI found no basis for investigating her disappearance as a kidnapping. She seemed content with her traveling life with Robert. So, what happened when she topped that slight rise in the path and left the sight of her friends? None of those questions has been answered.

INTENTIONALLY MISSING

On January 15, 1984, twenty-four-year-old Sherry Lyall Hart disappeared. She'd had a date that night, but he hadn't shown up. Then Sherry was just gone.

Her parents filed a missing-person report, but without evidence of foul play, authorities are often reluctant to follow up since most adults return home on their own. Sherry and her six-year-old daughter, April, had recently moved back in with her parents. A photograph of mother and daughter, taken a few years before Sherry disappeared, showed a little girl sitting in her mother's lap and grinning at the camera, both with shining heads of blonde hair. Sherry adored her daughter, and her family didn't believe the speculation that she'd run off to Florida or anywhere else.

Her father conducted his own search and found her car a few days later in West Jefferson. But still with no sign of foul play, investigators didn't dig any deeper—until almost a year later.

On December 10, authorities found skeletal remains at the bottom of a 1,200-foot cliff not far from Jumpinoff Rock, at the Ashe and Wilkes county line. Deputies were recovering a safe stolen from a convenience store when the sheriff saw skeletal hands embedded in the mud. The state medical examiner matched the remains to old X-rays and confirmed the body was Sherry's.

When investigators finally started asking questions, they learned she'd been seen that January night with two men she gone to high school with: Richard Bare and Jeffrey Burgess. She had dated Bare's brother for a time. When confronted with statements from other witnesses during his second interview with police, Jeffrey Burgess started talking. Bare and Burgess saw Sherry sitting in her car in a West Jefferson grocery store parking lot, apparently after her date didn't arrive. She accepted their invitation to cruise around with them in Bare's white Ford Mustang.

Later, when Sherry asked to pull off the road so she could relieve herself, Bare followed her into the woods and made a sexual advance. When Sherry said no, Bare got angry. She ran from the woods to the car and begged Burgess to protect her. Bare chased her, hitting her in the side of the head with his handgun. Burgess later said he was surprised the blow didn't knock her unconscious.

Bare told Burgess to drive from Idlewild Road to a bar not far from the Blue Ridge Parkway on the county line. Burgess pulled onto a turnoff that clung to the side of the mountain. Bare dragged the bleeding and groggy Sherry out of the car and told Burgess to drive down Highway 16 to the Moonshine Inn, turn around and come back. In the rearview mirror, Burgess saw the two walking in the direction of the bar, the guardrail the only thing between them and a steep drop off the mountain.

Burgess did as he was told and returned a few minutes later. When Bare climbed in the passenger seat of the Mustang, Sherry wasn't with him.

Steep drop at the Jumpinoff Rock parking area hints at dangerous terrain along the nearby Blue Ridge Parkway and Highway 16. *Photo by Cathy Pickens.*

Burgess didn't turn to look at Bare, but he asked what he'd done with her. "The bitch got what she deserved! She hung up, and then slid on down."

Burgess kept quiet for eleven months for fear Bare would make good on his threats to do something to him or his family. After her remains were found and he finally began talking, the information he gave investigators checked out. At the spot where he said Bare tried to attack Sherry in the woods, investigators found her checkbook and other scattered items, which helped corroborate his story.

In March 1985, fourteen months after Sherry disappeared, the two men were charged with her murder, arrested and taken to jails in separate counties: Burgess to Ashe County and Bare to Wilkes County.

In July, Bare escaped through an unlocked door, hid in the jail kitchen until the coast was clear and walked out the front door. The details of how he managed to escape have been examined, criticized and second-guessed. One of the Wilkes County jailers had been dating Bare's sister, and she sometimes visited her boyfriend while he was working. He and the other jailer on duty that night were soon no longer employed by the sheriff's office, but whether they helped Bare escape was never officially disclosed.

In a place where people knew Bare and knew about his arrest, how far could he get on foot? How could he escape with no money, beyond what might have been in his pocket for buying personal items at the jail? How far were family or friends willing to go to protect or aid him?

Jeff Burgess wasn't prosecuted for Sherry's death, although he served time for unrelated breaking and entering and drug violations. He agreed to testify against Bare, but that trial never took place. Burgess, a diabetic, died in 2012 at age forty-seven. Despite national coverage and a feature on *Unsolved Mysteries* that initially aired on October 14, 2008, Bare is still on the run.

According to his profile on the North Carolina SBI's most wanted list, Bare was born on July 6, 1964. He was a small man, five-foot-six and weighing 145 pounds, when he disappeared. He had a panther tattoo on his right forearm, brown hair and green eyes. The wanted bulletin noted that he might disguise himself as a woman.

In June 2002, district attorney Tom Horner—who represented Allegheny, Ashe, Wilkes and Yadkin Counties—sought a court order for the fingerprints of a man in Caldwell County. For case watchers, that move looked promising. Maybe authorities had found Richard Bare hiding close to home after all those years? The formal name of the document Horner filed was an Application for Nontestimonial Identification Order to obtain the prints of a man named Richard Presnell.

In a later interview, Presnell said that as soon as the SBI agent took the first print, he looked up and shook his head. "At that point, everyone started being really nice to me," Presnell said. But no explanation was ever made public or given to Presnell about what led the district attorney to suspect him. Presnell was told that Bare had a credit card in his name, but he never saw proof of that.

JOURNALIST LARRY J. GRIFFIN began writing about the case as a special reporter for *The Record* in Wilkes County and later posted the articles to the "Sherry Lyall Hart" Facebook page. The series eventually covered more than thirty articles and more than sixty thousand words. He posted photos from the recovery at the base of the cliff, family photos and annual birthday greetings to Sherry's daughter, April; interviewed anyone who would talk to him; and asked the page's growing number of followers to contact authorities to keep the case alive.

In 2018, the North Carolina Society of Historians presented Multimedia Awards to Larry J. Griffin and to April Billings for the "Sherry Lyall Hart" Facebook page and "its excellence for keeping this unresolved murder case in the public eye." The award judges' statement said, "Each of us became connected to the story of Sherry Hart through those articles, as much as feeling a connection with her daughter, April Billings. No longer was Sherry Hart a ghost of the past. Mr. Griffin has breathed new life into her memory and the search for her killer."

"I do think about it a lot," April told reporter Scott Sexton. "I always think and wonder if he might have walked in somewhere I was and been standing nearby and I just never knew it."

MEANT TO BE MISSING

Some go missing in the mountains by accident, and the mysteries persist. Some choose the mountains as the perfect place to disappear, hoping to remain a mystery.

William Bradford Bishop Jr. saw the Smoky Mountains as the perfect disappearing place. He left behind a horror for others to find when he apparently headed toward a new life for himself. Along the way, he traveled the length of North Carolina, finally abandoning his car just over the line in Tennessee, although maybe he crossed back over the ridge line to North Carolina to throw off his pursuers. That's part of the mystery.

On March 18, 1976, a man called park rangers to report what looked like an abandoned car in the parking lot at Elkmont, in the Great Smoky Mountains National Park about ten miles from Gatlinburg, Tennessee. The maroon Chevrolet station wagon was dirty and covered with brush.

The ranger found no keys hidden on the station wagon, although hikers sometimes leave a spare key balanced on a tire or attached with a magnet. He traced the license plate to Bradford Bishop's home address in Bethesda,

Maryland. That name and that address were already on Maryland authorities' radar: Bishop, his mother, his wife and their three sons had disappeared from their home. Given what they had found inside the sprawling house, investigators looking for Bishop didn't know if they were searching for him as a sixth victim or as the murderer.

BRAD BISHOP SPENT HIS career with the U.S. State Department. He earned a master's degree from Yale in African studies and a master's degree in Italian from Vermont's Middlebury College and spoke several languages. With his family, he had been stationed in Ethiopia, Botswana and Italy. He was a licensed pilot and an experienced outdoorsman who had enjoyed camping while in Africa, but he also wrestled with insomnia, alcoholism and depression. He was described as "intense and self-absorbed, prone to violent outbursts, and preferred a neat and orderly environment."

The thirty-nine-year-old economic affairs officer had been recently passed over for a promotion and was at a critical juncture in his career. He wasn't handling the professional setback well, and he indicated to some that his wife might have been counting on the promotion more than he was. The couple lived with his mother and their three sons, ranging in age from five to fourteen, in a spacious house with a large yard.

No one had seen or heard from anyone in the family after March 1. Brad Bishop had called his office to say he was sick with the flu. The two school-age sons hadn't gone to school that day. A few lights burned inside the house, but no one answered the door when neighbors stopped by. Police made a wellness check and found the house locked up tight, but the local post office said the Bishops usually put a hold on their mail if they would be out of town. A pile of mail in the mailbox and what looked like blood on the exterior steps gave police a reason to get inside the house.

Upstairs and down, in almost every room, police found dried pools and swaths of blood, as if objects had been dragged along the floor. They also found a bloody baseball bat but no bodies. Even Leo, the Bishops' golden retriever, was missing.

IN THE FIRE LOOKOUT tower near Columbia, North Carolina, Wilma Swain spotted smoke in the woods only about a mile from the tower. She notified forest ranger Ronald Brickhouse, and he soon radioed for Wilma to send the sheriff. She thought that he'd find a moonshine still in operation, something not unexpected in those woods. But that's not what he'd found. Even as the ranger stared at the burning vegetation, a gasoline can on fire and what looked like two bodies in a shallow pit, he had trouble taking in what he was seeing.

When the SBI investigators arrived in the remote piney woods near Eastern North Carolina's Albemarle Sound, they found that the pit held three more bodies: the two adults and three children were badly burned. The North Carolina medical examiner in Chapel Hill determined that four of the victims were beaten to death before the fire began; the older woman had also been struck but apparently died of a heart attack. Nothing was left to identify them except a well-worn pitchfork and a newer shovel with a partial price tag attached to the handle.

With help from the nearby Tyrrell Hardware Company, SBI agents traced the price sticker to the shovel's manufacturer and then to a hardware store in Bethesda, Maryland, but the shovel was a popular item—singling out the buyer proved impossible.

Tyrrell County dispatched a police bulletin seeking information on the five bodies located on March 2. The large number of victims quickly led to a matching missing-persons report. Now police were left wondering what happened to Brad Bishop and the dog.

In Jacksonville, North Carolina, less than 150 miles from the Tyrell County scene, a credit card receipt with handwriting matched to Bishop's showed that he'd bought camping gear at a sporting goods store the day after the family disappeared from Maryland.

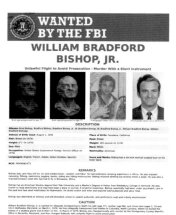

Wanted poster with age-enhanced images of Brad Bishop released thirty-seven years after he disappeared. *Released by the Federal Bureau of Investigation.*

State and federal authorities continued to collect charge card receipts showing his movement through North Carolina, but technology was not able to provide information quickly enough to catch up with Bishop and the maroon station wagon.

On March 18, the car was found abandoned in the Smoky Mountains. The FBI provided its crime lab and expertise to evaluate the car's contents. Canvas tarpaulins, blankets and the rear section of the station wagon were all covered with blood. Investigators knew that Leo was alive during the trip because they found a box of dog biscuits on the front floorboard and crumbs in the seat. Those who knew Bishop said he loved animals and wouldn't harm Leo. Did he let him out somewhere on his long trip from Maryland and through North Carolina?

In the car, they found a suitcase and men's clothing, a 12-gauge shotgun with ammunition, camping gear and a credit card receipt for gas from Columbia, North Carolina, close to where the bodies were found.

FBI agents and park rangers, with assistance from an FBI bloodhound named J. Edgar, fanned out from the car, trying to pick up Bishop's trail. They methodically searched the buildings in the Tennessee ghost town of Elkmont, close to the parking area. The early 1900s lumber town had transformed over the years into a rustic resort destination until the park service began acquiring property for the national park. The final private leases on the cottages expired in 1992. The park service's plans to restore the site to its pre-logging-days environment were thwarted by National Register of Historic Places designations on seventy of the buildings.

By the time of the search in 1976, some of the buildings were already badly deteriorated, but searchers had plenty of still-used weekend cottages

An Elkmont cabin, among those still used as vacation homes when Bishop disappeared in 1976. *Courtesy of Joel Kramer via Creative Commons and licensed under CC BY 2.0.*

One of the cabins at Elkmont, now abandoned. *Courtesy of Joel Kramer via Creative Commons and licensed under CC BY 2.0.*

to check. They found no sign that Bishop had broken into any, although J. Edgar alerted on the steps and porch of one of the cottages.

The search lasted almost four days. They knew that Bishop had a Serax prescription for depression, and they hadn't ruled out the possibility he'd come to the mountains to kill himself. However, they found no sign of his body. They questioned hikers and campers in the area. A group of Eagle Scouts reported a conversation with a couple who said they'd camped one night near a man wearing street clothes. He was headed toward Newfound Gap, a drivable pass over the Smokies into North Carolina—coincidentally, not far from where Polly Melton disappeared five years later at Deep Creek.

Had Bishop died by suicide somewhere off the trails? Had he hiked out to a road and caught a ride? Did he have an accomplice? Had he acquired a fake passport sometime before the murders and left the country?

Bishop's work experience in Africa and Europe made it plausible that he could hide there, and later sightings—in Stockholm and Sorrento—by people who personally knew Bishop suggested that he may have left the country and set up another life.

Bishop was indicted for the murders in Maryland in absentia. When *Unsolved Mysteries* first televised Bishop's case in 1980, the broadcast generated tips, as did later rebroadcasts, but he has never been captured. In 2014, the DNA from cigarette butts found in his car was checked against an unidentified body in Alabama, but there was no match.

In 2021, A CASE that already had plenty of strange twists got stranger. Kathy Gillcrist's cousin in Maine—whom Kathy located using a consumer DNA testing service—was helping Kathy search for her birth parents. A coastal North Carolina resident, Kathy had been adopted into a loving family, but as with many adoptees, the differences between her and her adopted family made her wonder what her birth family was like, how much of her personality was due to nature and how much from nurture. The two cousins quickly located Kathy's mother, but finding her father took a little longer.

In a later interview with Ohio public television station WCET, Kathy said her cousin contacted her one day: "I'm only going to give you his name."

"Is it someone famous?"

"Um, yeah."

When Kathy found the story of Bradford Bishop online and saw that he was one of the FBI's most wanted fugitives, she laughed. "We have a great sense of humor in my adoptive family, and I thought, 'Of course, my father's a murderer.'" Kathy's birth mother had arranged for her adoption in 1957, before Bishop married and had his three sons.

Kathy wrote a book about her experiences as an adoptee and her unusual family connection, but the discovery provided no answers to the mystery of what happened to Brad Bishop in 1976.

BAD MEN

THE ORE KNOB MINE MURDERS

Hell's Angels and the Outlaws. Beginning in the 1970s, the nationally known bad-actor motorcycle gangs—or motorcycle clubs, as they called themselves—had a big presence in North Carolina, especially in Charlotte and Durham. Like a mature church starting a new congregation by "planting" a new church, the clubs recruited new members in new areas. Unlike church members, though, these new congregants were expected to pass stringent, violent tests—including murder—and they were expected to establish drug and prostitution networks in their new home and take over, or take out, any competitors.

The Outlaws from Chicago—where the motorcycle club originated—had direct ties to the Western North Carolina club, and local rumors said the club had ties to a Chicago crime boss. They reportedly moved large amounts of marijuana, cocaine, hashish and Canadian Valium, called "Blues," as well as weapons that needed to be taken somewhere far away from the scene of a crime. They controlled much of the prostitution in the area, but their main moneymaker was drugs.

In 1981, a decade before cheap crack made cocaine readily available and ignited a drug crime wave across North Carolina and the United States, a small group of men controlled Western North Carolina's drug business, with an unusual way of handling those who double-crossed them. Murder was an easy solution, as long as you had somewhere handy to hide the bodies. And they did.

Federal investigators suspected that one of the operational centers for the drug trade was an Asheville bar on Swannanoa River Road called Sarge's Lounge, just down the hill from an X-rated drive-in theater. Proprietor Paul "Sarge" Harris, more than six feet tall and retired military, had a sharp eye for spotting cops or infiltrators.

As federal authorities were considering how to get inside Sarge's operation, Joseph Vines walked into the Alcohol, Tobacco and Firearms (ATF) office in Asheville's Federal Building. He came to collect his paycheck for an undercover job he'd done for an agent in another state.

Joe Vines had worked as a paid confidential informant for a decade. He wrestled with his reservations about his life as "half-crook, half-cop," but he also had his reasons for wanting to put drug dealers out of business. His mother had moved him to Florida when he was in elementary school, along with however many of his seventeen brothers were still living at home. He'd grown up with other kids who lived on the fringe, dealing in drugs and stolen goods to pay for the drugs. That was easy money and an accepted part of his life—until Maria, a beautiful seventeen-year-old girl he cared about, got hooked and damaged her brain on STP when she thought she was taking mescaline. A popular street drug for a time, "Serenity, Tranquility and Peace," as it was nicknamed, had nothing to do with the engine additives. It was more powerful but slower acting than mescaline, so users often overdosed by accident. He had also watched an eleven-year-old boy vomit until he died after taking an overdose.

Those two incidents were enough for Joe Vines. He went from hating snitches to becoming one, helping police build the case to put away the dealer who sold those drugs to his friends.

At six-foot-six, 240 pounds and bald with a large mustache, Joe Vines commanded attention. He'd honed his craft as an informant and had helped investigators build cases in several cities, including Tampa, Cleveland and Fayetteville, and a case against some Hell's Angels in Chicago.

ATF agent Thomas Chapman recognized Joe's potential as soon as he walked through the door. Vines had a solid reputation with the agents he'd worked with, and he looked the part. Chapman asked if he was interested in working in the Asheville area and took him to meet FBI agent Thomas Frye. The agent needed someone who could fit in at Sarge's bar, set up some drug buys and get to know some of the bikers who hung out there.

Joe had no trouble fitting in. In fact, within a matter of days, Sarge hired him to work as a bouncer at the bar. It didn't take long for Joe to be included in the kinds of activities that would interest the federal investigators. One particular activity would change his life.

In mid-December, Sarge asked Joe—he called him "Kojak" because of his bald head—if he was willing to put a scare in a guy who owed him money. As long as it was just to scare a guy, Joe said sure. Sarge introduced him to two men in the back room at the bar. Alan Ray Hattaway moved drugs and did hits for the Outlaws Club. With his scraggly beard, foul language and vicious past, he was the picture of a true biker tough. Gary Miller—a big, quiet man—also dealt drugs and was suspected in a murder.

The next day, December 21, Hattaway took Joe to call on Lonnie Gamboa, who was a surprising contrast to the rough, unkempt, uneducated Outlaws. Hattaway told Gamboa he had to come up with $120,000 for his share of the drugs the gang had brought to Asheville. Gamboa insisted he only owed $30,000, and he offered property, a van and a payment plan to get them their money. That didn't satisfy Hattaway.

Hattaway and Joe drove Gamboa to Candler to pick up some of the unsold drugs and to Atlanta to retrieve some rings Gamboa had been responsible for getting sized for Hattaway. One was a Ku Klux Klan ring; the other was a skull and crossbones studded with diamonds and a ruby mouth—the ring of an Outlaws hitman.

On December 23, Hattaway called Joe and told him to get in touch with Gamboa. He wanted the deeds for Gamboa's land and house trailer transferred into Hattaway's name. He also wanted Joe to pick up Gamboa and make sure that Gamboa had gone to the courthouse to get a copy of the trial transcript from the Moffitt Branch shootout.

Hattaway's concerns about the transcript and the Moffitt Branch case were mysteries to Joe, but playing the role of loyal sidekick, he couldn't ask too many questions or act too curious. He could only watch and listen, trying to piece together the plot that swirled around him.

When Gamboa got in Joe's car, Gamboa's only concern was that he'd had to pay $370 for the transcript, but he had it in an envelope. While Joe drove to Sarge's, Hattaway sat in the back of the car reading the transcript. Hattaway wanted to find out if Gamboa had lied to him about how he'd testified in the Moffitt Branch case.

At Sarge's, Miller joined them, also upset with Gamboa—at the time, another mystery to Joe. The men bound Gamboa's hands and loaded him in the car. They drove toward Morganton, then along the Blue Ridge Parkway to a paved road, then onto a dirt road and past an old wooden house with motorcycles parked on the porch to a garage behind the house. Gamboa had to answer in person to Paul "Papa" Bare, the "big man."

In Bare's garage, Joe had a scare. As soon as they arrived, Miller asked Bare to check on some names for him, and one of those names was Joseph Vines. Joe hadn't used his real name when he started working for Sarge. In the garage, Joe maintained his stoic composure, as any hint that he was a police informant would be a death sentence for him. That Miller knew his real name indicated a leak somewhere among the investigators, someone who talked to Miller.

Bare picked up the phone and had a hushed conversation. Fortunately, Joe won some extra time. Bare couldn't answer Miller's question because "the machine" was down. Joe knew that Bare's phone call went to a cop somewhere, who was checking official databases at the gangster's request. This operation was well connected.

Joe had to put those worries on the back burner so he could pay attention to what was playing out around Gamboa. After threatening and cajoling from Gamboa the location of drugs, money and other valuables, Bare said they were taking him to see the "big boss." *Another big boss?* Joe wondered.

"You come, too, Kojak. We'll take the back roads, but we'll have to walk part of the way through some brush and stuff. We might need you." Joe wasn't feeling well—either from fear or a flu that would stick with him for two weeks. He tried to back out, but Hattaway challenged him, "Sarge said we could count on you." Joe had to join them.

Miller, Joe and a blindfolded Gamboa crowded into a pickup truck driven by Bare. Joe pulled his hat over his eyes, as Bare ordered, so he couldn't see where they were going. Hattaway followed in his own car as they left Papa Bare's garage. It was the early morning of Christmas Eve 1981.

They drove through the dark to a rough, graveled section off a narrow two-lane road. Hattaway also pulled off and parked. He would wait as lookout. The four men in the truck drove a short distance off the main road and then walked uphill until they reached a tall chain link fence.

Joe didn't know it at the time, but the fence surrounded what remained of the Ore Knob Mine in Ashe County. Starting in 1855, the mine produced primarily copper but also some silver and gold. In the late 1800s, the mine was the largest and richest ore producer in the world and continued to operate, off and on, as an important economic driver in the region until 1962.

Joe didn't know the place or the history. He only knew that it was dark and required them to walk uphill for a distance through brambles and pine

Left: Sign for Ore Knob Mine Road. The once-productive copper mine has been filled and the land reclaimed. *Photo by Cathy Pickens.*

Right: Highway marker commemorating the history of Ore Knob Mine. *Photo by Cathy Pickens.*

saplings. The wind was bitter cold and threatening snow. Joe later said the climb up a small hill took about five or ten minutes. Gamboa was still blindfolded, which made navigating through the underbrush difficult. Joe helped him along.

At the top of the hill, Bare guided Gamboa through an opening cut four or five feet high through the chain fence. Bare then motioned with a shotgun for Joe to follow Gamboa. Once the two were inside the fence, Joe could make out an enormous hole. He couldn't tell how deep it was. He only knew that Miller and Bare both held serious weapons and that Miller had questions about some guy named Joseph Vines.

Miller waved his gun, motioning for Joe to push Gamboa into the hole. Later, Joe described the thoughts racing through his head. He had no idea how deep the hole was or what was inside. He didn't have much space where he stood, maybe only three feet between the fence and the edge.

He knew if he pushed Gamboa, he could be the next one to disappear. If he didn't push Gamboa, they would shoot him. Either way, he had a good chance of ending up at the bottom of a dark hole. His only chance of avoiding being killed himself was to do what they told him.

At Bare's trial, Joe said, "When I tapped Mr. Gamboa on the shoulder, he took a step forward and went into the hole." At that point, what was already a nightmare went sideways. Gamboa's ankle got tangled in a root about two or three feet down inside the hole, and he just hung there, still alive and hollering. Bare told Joe to pull him out. Joe was afraid of falling or being pulled down. Bare handed him a large tree limb through the opening in the fence.

Gamboa, still hanging upside down, couldn't reach the limb, and his leg was broken. Bare screamed, making it clear that the consequences were bad if Gamboa didn't try. He grabbed the limb and Joe pulled him up. Bare motioned with the shotgun for Joe to push him again. Gamboa, still blindfolded, disappeared into the dark.

Joe scrambled back through the slit in the fence. Bare ordered him and Miller to throw rocks into the hole, to make sure Gamboa had fallen to the bottom. They heard the rocks hit but no other sounds.

"He went down easier than the one two weeks ago," Miller said. "That makes twenty-two."

"You're wrong," said Bare. "That makes twenty-three."

Joe consistently maintained that until he first stepped through the fence and saw the hole, he had no idea what they had planned for Gamboa that night. Until Miller's comment, Joe also didn't know that the mine was a hiding place for multiple killings. He had signed on to help make some drug cases, not to be involved in something like this. He had also been around people like Bare and Miller long enough to know that they would have no reservations about making him disappear forever.

Joe Vines knew the risks that night were real, but he didn't learn until later that his act of obedience proved his worth to the Outlaws and earned him a high place in the "family" as a hitman who could settle scores and collect debts for the club.

Vines also learned that night, after the trip to Ore Knob Mine, that Bare's drug operation wasn't small. Bare took Vines up the hill behind his garage and showed him the airplane they used to bring in quantities of marijuana. Vines also saw the old garbage truck, large cans and reinforced trash bags they used to haul or hide quantities of pot.

Joe knew he had to get in touch with Thomas Chapman, the ATF agent who first introduced him to those investigating Sarge and Papa Bare. He had to let Chapman know what had happened and what his role was. He knew he'd had no choice but to push Gamboa into that mine shaft. He'd had no other option, but to protect himself in the eyes of the law, he had to let Chapman know.

It was Christmas Eve. While criminals don't take holidays off, federal agents do. As soon as Joe could separate himself from Bare and the others, he started calling and leaving messages.

Finally, on January 5, he talked to Chapman. That same day, Joe got another shock. He was riding with Miller when a patrol car pulled them over. The officers arrested Miller for kidnapping Thomas Forester, another Asheville drug dealer, and his girlfriend, Betty Callahan. A patrolman at the scene told Joe he didn't have any reason to hold him, and another officer drove him home.

Joe didn't know it at the time, but Forester also disappeared into the Ore Knob Mine shaft, on December 13. He had no way to make the connection when he was standing in Papa Bare's garage, but he'd seen a calendar on the wall with two dates circled in red: December 13 and December 23, the dates Forester and Gamboa were taken to Ore Knob Mine.

Investigators later found Betty Callahan alive and learned she'd been given an option: she could go to Chicago and be forced to work as a prostitute or she could share her boyfriend Forester's fate, whatever that might be. She chose Chicago, where she worked for six weeks before she escaped.

ON JANUARY 6, AFTER hearing Joe Vines's story, officials blocked off access to the mine shaft. At this point, the story got even stranger. Already rife with motorcycle gang members, drug dealers, callous murder, a body dump in a mine shaft and sex trafficking, the case now got an unlikely hero: a country music singer turned stuntman, the Nashville Flash—at least, that was the name on his Tennessee driver's license.

Before the Flash offered his help, authorities tried several ways to check out Joe's story about the body—or bodies—in the mine. Ashe County's Sheriff Waddell scouted the area and called in mining authorities for their expertise. The special camera and lights to be lowered into the shaft didn't arrive until January 12. Old maps suggested that the search should be straightforward, but the camera couldn't move easily among the debris and got only limited views. A mining expert said the soft soil around the shaft opening and the litter-strewn interior made conditions too dangerous to explore.

The people who'd elected the sheriff wanted him to get to the bottom of what had happened, literally. And plenty of rock climbers and cave crawlers volunteered for the job. Finally, disguised in a mask and helmet to protect his identity from the drug dealers and bikers, the Nashville Flash arrived on the scene. Not only did he have a career in country music, but the Flash did stunt work, mostly as charity fundraisers. Before Ore Knob, his big headliner act was his escape from a Flaming Tee-Pee of Death.

Attached to a cable dangling from a crane, the Flash's slight frame descended a few hundred feet into the hole. He carried with him a gas detector and a flood light.

The mine had been out of service since 1962 and was more difficult to navigate than expected. In those twenty years, it accumulated everything from animal carcasses to building debris and car parts. On the fifth trip into the mine, the crane's cable lowered the Flash along with Asheville police officer Roger Buckner and Ashe County sheriff's captain Gene Goss. (Goss was later elected sheriff and involved in the hunt for Sherry Hart's killer.) After an hour of working with picks and shovels, the men freed Gamboa's frozen body. He was still blindfolded, just as Vines described.

Buckner spotted Forester's body not far from Gamboa's, and they brought it to the surface later that evening. Both bodies had frozen into contorted postures. Captain Goss said he'd seen no sign of other bodies on his two trips at the end of the crane cable. Perhaps some had been dumped years ago and were covered by dirt and debris, but he thought the other bodies Miller and Bare mentioned must be other crimes in other places, not bodies dumped in that shaft.

The two bodies were recovered on January 25, 1982. The shaft was filled in and the ground leveled in February.

For the three gang members, murder charges were added to their existing kidnapping charges. Bare, who'd been out on bond, was returned to jail. Miller and Hattaway went on the run. Ironically, both were captured the day the jury returned its verdict in Bare's case. Agents found a now heavier, toothless Miller living in the Castlebridge Campground near Lenoir, North Carolina. Hattaway turned himself in to agents in Newport, Tennessee.

PAUL "PAPA" BARE'S TRIAL for Gamboa's murder was held in the courthouse in Jefferson. Built in 1904, it now houses the Museum of Ashe County History and is listed in the National Register of Historic Places.

Bare's defense attorney, Edwin Marger of Atlanta, wasn't well known in Ashe County but had defended others charged with large-scale drug offenses, including the brother-in-law of "Baby Doc" Duvalier, Haiti's dictator. Marger's linen suits and private plane didn't sit well with the locals, but he was there to do a job. Most critical among his tasks was discrediting the prosecution's chief witness, Joseph Vines.

The old Ashe County Courthouse, built in 1904, now houses the Museum of Ashe County History. *Courtesy of Jblevins47 via Wikimedia Commons.*

The trial opened on June 2, 1982. ATF agent Thomas Chapman was the prosecution's first witness and the defense's opening gambit in discrediting Joe. During cross-examination, Marger intently questioned the agent about when and how Joe tried to get in touch with him after the incident at the mine. The defense contended that Vines was a party to the murder, not an innocent man coerced into pushing Gamboa into the pit and not a man who kept his government handlers informed about what he was doing.

Was Joe a good guy forced to do something bad, or a bad guy who just added one more item to his list of misdeeds? In news accounts of Bare's trial, no consensus developed on his character or motivation.

Agent Chapman believed that Joe was trustworthy, a good man, and he testified to that. Marger clearly needed to convince the jury that he was a bad guy, that he'd acted without Bare's coercion. Marger spent a lot of time trying to discredit Joe as a snitch, telling the jury, "We have here a study of a man who has made his living as a perpetual Judas Iscariot betraying those around him."

Marger also tried to argue that Gamboa had been killed before he went into the mine shaft, to strengthen his argument that Vines hadn't simply pushed him. Dr. Page Hudson, the state's chief medical examiner, didn't yield on that point. In his opinion, Gamboa was alive when he fell and took a few breaths before dying of injuries from the two-hundred-foot fall.

When the two bodies first arrived in Chapel Hill for autopsy, the bodies had to thaw for a day before the pathologist could examine them. Both bodies demonstrated the kinds of lacerations and internal damage expected in such a long fall. In Gamboa's case, Dr. Hudson noted a head injury from a severe blow with a narrow instrument but found that consistent with hitting a rock or piece of wood inside the mine shaft. The head injury and the other trauma happened close together in time.

Dr. Hudson's testimony presented a powerful rebuttal to the defense claim that Joe killed Gamboa before he threw him into the mine. At autopsy, Dr. Hudson noted a tear in Gamboa's lung and blood aspirated into the lower lobe, which "would have only taken a breath or two after the impact."

Later, the jury at Hattaway's trial for Forester's murder heard testimony that Hattaway said "he had to fight the son-of-a-bitch he put in the mine a couple of weeks ago," indicating that Forester was also alive when he went into the shaft. Dr. Hudson's autopsy findings also confirmed that.

Despite Marger's efforts during the two-week trial to free him, the hometown jury sentenced Papa Bare to life imprisonment, which, at the time, made him eligible to seek parole in twenty years. Reports at the time of trial said Marger couldn't believe the outcome. A small-town North Carolina jury had handed him his first loss in thirty years.

In March 1983, after Bare's trial, an Ashe County grand jury refused to indict Joe Vines in Gamboa's murder. However, when the trial of Miller and Hattaway started on February 7, 1984, Vines wasn't around to testify. He'd gone into hiding in Florida, legitimately afraid of reprisals from the motorcycle gang. Did public sentiment change, or did his federal handlers no longer have any need for him? Whatever the reason, on February 16, a county grand jury indicted Joe Vines for Gamboa's kidnapping and murder.

That indictment and Joe's trial raised important questions about the role of police informants—and the protections owed them in their work. In later years, serious questions would arise about FBI informants using their status as a shield for their own criminal activity. The most high-profile case was James "Whitey" Bulger, an informant for Boston FBI agent John Connolly. As Bulger's handler, Connolly got tips about Italian mob figures and, in exchange, turned a blind eye to the violence and murder Bulger ordered in the South Boston Irish mob he ran.

Over the years, Bulger got more brazen. In 1994, Connolly alerted him that agents were poised to arrest him. Bulger disappeared and stayed on the run with his longtime girlfriend until his capture in 2011.

When Connolly was sentenced to forty years for his role, he defended his actions to a *Boston Globe* reporter: "We got 42 stone criminals by giving up two stone criminals. What's your return on investment there? Show me a businessman who wouldn't do that?"

Connolly was referring to Bulger's torture and murder of two informants, measured against the number—outside Bulger's own gang—that his tips helped arrest. Ironically, when Bulger agreed to work with Connolly, he didn't want to be called a confidential informant or CI, in agency parlance—or a rat, in gang terms. He wanted to be referred to as Connolly's "strategist."

When news broke in 1995 about Connolly and Bulger, the use of informants and their potential for abuse caused a firestorm of official and public protest. FBI agents were then required to track the number of times they gave their informants permission to break the law. After all, in gathering information on criminal activity, informants aren't hanging out at choir practice, and they aren't choir boys themselves.

The crimes the agency considered permissible were mostly buying and selling drugs or crimes related to illegal drug activity. A 2011 report showed that, on average, fifteen crimes per day were permitted by FBI agents nationwide. The argument was that, without allowing these smaller crimes, the bigger fish would get away.

In 1984, the uproar over doing crooked things to catch criminals hadn't surfaced yet. But in the mountains, as on the streets of any city, the culture against snitches was strong. On the other hand, without Joe Vines, two murders would have gone unpunished, and the drug ring that spawned that violence would have continued operating in the Asheville area.

The jury in Bare's trial found Joe credible and took less than half an hour to convict Bare of first-degree murder. In Joe's trial, the evidence against him came from unexpected sources. An undercover police officer claimed that Joe approached him and solicited him about doing a drug deal.

The most shocking testimony came from a man who claimed Joe asked him to help with a hit on Gamboa. However, according to the witness, that solicitation happened almost a month before Vines said he'd first heard Gamboa's name.

On cross-examination, Vines's defense attorney pointed to inconsistencies in the witness's testimony and to his questionable past. "Is it true," he asked, "that when you first met Vines, your main income was from selling the gold you took from the teeth of corpses in a mausoleum?" The witness refused to answer to avoid incriminating himself.

When Joe was asked why he didn't just call the Asheville police when he couldn't get in touch with federal agents over the holidays after Gamboa's murder, Joe said he didn't trust the police. He had legitimate reasons to suspect that some bent cops worked on the local forces after hearing Bare phone someone asking to have some names—including his own—checked out in a database. He'd also seen officers come by Sarge's Lounge to pick up money.

Although the tooth-stealing chief witness against him had a less than sterling reputation, that didn't help Joe. The jury took two days, apparently debating voluntary manslaughter versus murder. They found him guilty of murder but recommended life rather than death, citing the credible threat to his life and his good work as an informant. Joe would be eligible for parole in twenty years or less. He was placed in protective custody under an alias because of the very real risks he faced inside a prison. He earned three college degrees while incarcerated and was later released with another identity.

Paul Bare died in prison in 1989 at age forty-nine. When he was freed, Gary Miller didn't stay out long; he was re-arrested for another crime soon after his release. Alan Hattaway was released in 2010.

HISTORY FADES FROM MEMORY and becomes difficult to resurrect unless someone works to preserve it. Author Rose M. Haynes wrote that a local headline, "Man Pushed Alive into Ore Knob Mine Shaft—23 Bodies Rumored to Be in Mine," stayed with her for years. She knew that someone had to write about how drugs and the violence they brought affected the region she called home. As a reporter, she covered Joseph Vines's 1984 trial for the *Journal-Patriot*. She acknowledged the generosity of Ashe County sheriff Eugene Goss in sharing information about the investigation. She spent two years hand-copying Paul Bare's trial transcript at the Ashe County courthouse. Trial materials aren't kept forever, and the transcript was later destroyed. Her work—and her book—preserved that record.

She also contacted Joseph Vines in prison, and he agreed to talk to her, provided she took measures to protect his identity and location; he had a price on his head, even in prison. He continued to answer her questions after his release, but he wouldn't let her know where he was living.

Rose Haynes said she was motivated by the threat of drugs but also by questions about what the government owes those who work as informants. Without them, cases wouldn't be made. And without Rose's work, this story could easily have been lost in the continual accumulation of newer cases.

CURTIS SHEDD

A small southern town in the 1950s would seem an unlikely place for a tragic case of multiple rape and murder. Those kinds of crimes would become more common later and in more distant, metropolitan places where faceless violence could be expected. But in a hot August in 1950, a local man brought that kind of violence to a family in Walhalla, South Carolina, tragedy that became forever associated with Western North Carolina.

Curtis Shedd met John Boyter at a post–World War II veteran's training school operated near Walhalla, and the two became friends. Boyter likely didn't know much about Shedd's background, other than their shared experiences of the war and the training school, but Shedd had recently been released from his second prison term for robbery.

On August 3, 1950, Shedd and Boyter were riding around Walhalla in Shedd's car. Later that afternoon, Shedd was alone when he stopped by Boyter's home to pick up the two Boyter daughters—Johnnie Mae, age fourteen, and Jo Ann, age eight—to join their dad for a car ride into the mountains. Shedd promised the family a trip to a circus in Clayton, Georgia.

The boundaries of North Carolina, South Carolina and Georgia all meet about thirty miles north of Walhalla. Soon after Shedd picked up the girls, a man in Satulah, Georgia, about eight miles outside Highlands, North Carolina, found Boyter's body in the woods near the post office, along the road from Walhalla. The father had been beaten and killed with a shotgun blast. When authorities learned that Shedd was last seen with Boyter and his family, they picked him up for questioning.

Shedd's multiple versions of events changed before and during his trial, obscuring what really happened. At first, he denied knowing anything about the missing girls and their murdered father. One account noted that "under a grueling interrogation," he eventually admitted he raped and strangled the girls. After he lured their father away for a drive in his newly refurbished car, Shedd killed him and went back to Walhalla to pick up the girls. He took them across the state line, where their bodies were later found near Highlands.

T.W. Reynolds, who interviewed locals and captured stories of the Highlands area in his books, recounted one of Shedd's many and varied accounts. The girls were killed about five miles outside Highlands, he said, on Highway 106 heading toward Dillard, the site of the town dump in the 1950s and 1960s. Reynolds wrote that the girls were killed "right where the strawberries grow," their bodies left there for at least ten days, until Shedd agreed to bring law enforcement to the scene.

After word got around that Shedd had been arrested, a reported crowd of four thousand people gathered outside the Walhalla jail. Some were calling for blood. The sheriff enlisted the support of fifty South Carolina National Guardsmen to keep the peace. A local newspaper reported, "The local sheriff told the crowd to 'go on home and let law and order take its course.' He added that he begged the men to 'pray and read your Bibles' and then come back if they thought it was God's way."

After some negotiation among South Carolina, North Carolina and Georgia about jurisdiction, Shedd was transferred to jail in Georgia, where he was charged with John Boyter's murder. Eventually, authorities chose to first try him for the deaths of the two girls in Macon County, North Carolina. That trial was held in Franklin.

A jury was selected and brought in from Jackson County to hear the case, to avoid the local publicity and high feeling about the murders of the two children.

Woody Wilson, a Georgia State Bureau of Investigation agent, started working the case as soon as Boyter's body was found near Satulah. At the

F-5   COURT HOUSE, FRANKLIN, N. C.

Vintage postcard of the old Macon County Courthouse in Franklin, scene of Curtis Shedd's trial. *Courtesy of Durwood Barbour Collection of North Carolina Postcards, UNC, and Asheville Post Card Company.*

Macon County trial, he testified that Shedd went with officers to the site near Highlands, where he'd dumped the bodies, and demonstrated how he killed the oldest girl. The agent also testified that Shedd told several stories that changed over time.

Mrs. Boyter testified that she and her husband thought Shedd was taking their family to the circus, but that instead, he had attacked her and disappeared with her daughters.

During his trial, Curtis Shedd's frail wife sat beside him and "cried throughout most of the proceedings." Shedd didn't testify, and the only defense presented on his behalf hinted at mental illness. In his closing argument, Shedd's defense attorney said, "Look at him…sitting there chewing gum like he was at a Sunday picnic. Does he look like he is in his right mind?'"

The prosecutor argued that Shedd was the one who'd committed this "damnable crime" and called the defense's attempts to claim the jury should consider Shedd's mental condition as nothing but "novel injections of insanity." Summarizing what the jury had heard of Shedd, he said, "He is either the most foolish or the smartest man I have ever met."

On December 14, 1950, the jury deliberated for only an hour and convicted Shedd with no recommendation for mercy, which meant a death sentence. At those words, Mrs. Shedd sobbed even harder. To the end and for his own reasons, Shedd admitted he'd killed John Boyter, but he later refused to admit he'd killed the girls. In the saga of Shedd's ever-changing stories, he claimed that Boyter killed his own daughters. No one who knew Boyter believed he could harm them.

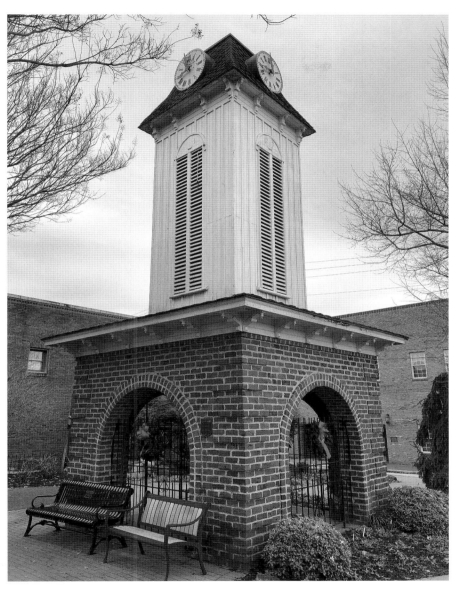

Tower from the 1881 Macon County Courthouse, placed on the town square when the building was demolished in 1972. *Courtesy of Warren LeMay via Wikimedia Commons.*

According to the *Sylva Herald & Ruralite*, after the hour-long deliberation and verdict, "When asked why they deliberated so long, the juror said they 'were meditating to make sure we were doing the right thing.'"

Governor Kerr Scott refused to stay the execution, scheduled for Good Friday, March 23, 1951. Shedd was executed in the gas chamber at North Carolina's Central Prison, sharing the small chamber with another man. Both men were baptized the day before their executions. A news report said that Shedd took his seat and "eyed his guards surlily" in the moments before the cyanide pellets dropped.

T.W. Reynolds noted that the little girls' family didn't have money for fancy headstones on their graves. Because Curtis Shedd served in the military, his grave—at the Long Creek Baptist Church Graveyard in South Carolina—had a military marker.

THE MOONSHINERS

Residents of Western North Carolina didn't invent the distilling of spirits. They brought that expertise with them from England, Scotland, Ireland, Wales and Germany. In sheltered mountain hollows with plenty of fresh water and little level ground for farming crops, the Europeans who settled the region did their part in perfecting the art of distilling, using primarily corn and sometimes barley.

In the 1800s, those who operated liquor stills did so mostly to supply family and friends. By the late 1800s, though, the federal government had taken an interest in those activities. The government first taxed distilled liquor in 1791 at the behest of Alexander Hamilton. In the late 1800s, the expenses of the Civil War prompted a more vigorous effort to collect taxes, which met with deep protest among mountain people accustomed to a live-and-let-live life removed from government interference.

On mountainous terrain, boundaries are difficult to discern, so moonshiners passed easily between Georgia and North and South Carolina, either in search of markets or to hide out when pursuers got too close. As one example, Lewis Redmond, known in those states as "King of the Moonshiners," started in North Carolina's Swain and Transylvania Counties in the 1830s and ended his days across the state line in Walhalla, South Carolina, employing his skills as a maker of quality liquor as head of the federal distillery.

The passage of Prohibition in 1920 increased both the lucrativeness of cooking liquor and the vehemence of government policing. When

The NASCAR Hall of Fame and museum in Charlotte. *Courtesy of Ken Lund via Creative Commons and licensed under CC BY-SA 2.0.*

Prohibition outlawed the manufacture, transportation and sale of liquor, business for mountain moonshiners boomed. They had honed their skills for generations, they didn't much like the government telling them what they could and couldn't do and they certainly didn't like paying taxes. They were ready and able to supply thirsty drinkers.

The myth of the moonshiner couldn't exist without the moonshine "runners" who transported the liquor from hidden stills to more lucrative urban markets. Model A and other early Fords were ideal as runners. A car had to be ubiquitous enough to pass without notice on the highway and be able to accommodate a stronger suspension so the car didn't sag from the weight or sway too much when moving at high speeds, and it needed a large trunk space. The Ford engine could be altered to provide more speed while hauling as much as eight hundred pounds of liquor and handling a 180-degree spin to switch direction should a revenue agent get too close.

When Prohibition ended, those modified cars were the genesis of what became NASCAR and professional stock car racing. The bootleg runners took their driving and car-modifying skills onto dirt tracks, testing themselves and their cars in races against one another rather than against federal agents. The best known was Junior Johnson, who served eleven months in a federal prison, although he was quick to point out that he was arrested at his daddy's still. No agent ever caught him on the road. In 2010, he was inducted in the first class of the NASCAR Hall of Fame in Charlotte.

The mountains weren't the only haven for bootleggers or moonshiners, but the legends around them have persisted and grown long after the cooking of corn liquor became legal (and even hip) in some states.

MURDER IN TWO STATES

In 1892, two friends, William Hall and Andrew Bryson, worked a still together in the mountains outside Murphy—the same mountains that would hide Olympic Park bomber Eric Rudolph one hundred years later.

Somehow, their still disappeared one day, and each looked at the other as the reason it was gone. Hall recruited John Dockery to help him find Bryson and teach him a lesson. The confrontation between the three men took place high on a ridge. A shot from Hall's rifle felled Bryson. The case would have disappeared, just as the still had done, with little evidence left behind—except for an oddity that led to two court appeals, a new state statute and some creative lawbreaking in the years to come.

When Hall and Dockery were arrested for Bryson's death, their lawyers raised an interesting question about whether they could be prosecuted in North Carolina. The mountain ridge ran along the border between North Carolina and Tennessee, and Hall fired the shot with his feet firmly on North Carolina soil. Bryson, though, was standing in Tennessee when the shot killed him. Which state had jurisdiction?

The North Carolina judge and jury ignored the boundary question and found Hall and Dockery guilty of murder. The two were sentenced to hang, but in April 1894, the North Carolina Supreme Court overturned their convictions. The court said that the crime took place where Arthur Bryson fell, that the bullet sent across the line, figuratively speaking, carried the shooter and his intentions with it. So it was a Tennessee case.

Later that year, the North Carolina Supreme Court heard a second appeal and held that the state could not detain the two men as "fugitives from justice" to allow Tennessee to try them. "A person cannot be said to flee from a place where he has never actually been," the court said. "One who has never fled cannot be a fugitive."

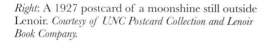

Above: An eighty-gallon moonshine still in North Carolina. *Courtesy of UNC Postcard Collection and Asheville Post Card Company.*

Right: A 1927 postcard of a moonshine still outside Lenoir. *Courtesy of UNC Postcard Collection and Lenoir Book Company.*

While the U.S. Constitution provided for extradition of those who committed crimes and fled to another state, North Carolina had not yet passed a statute that allowed for extradition from its boundaries to another state. Until the state legislature chose to act, the court said it could only enforce the law as it existed—or didn't exist, in this case.

This case was part of a series of legal wranglings trying to work out where state law ended and federal law began. States have jurisdiction over most criminal acts. The federal government can only pass laws forbidding criminal activity if specifically spelled out in the U.S. Constitution (such as treason) or if the criminal activity takes place across state lines (in interstate commerce). During Prohibition and with the rise of gangster activity during the Great Depression, states began passing laws that allowed governors to seek extradition of criminals who fled to other states, and the federal government became involved in crimes not limited to a single state—crimes such as kidnapping or bootlegging or robbery, where the criminals fled across state lines to escape capture or prosecution.

As in other states, the North Carolina legislature didn't address crimes that crossed state lines until the 1930s, passing a law that provided for "such cases, even though the accused was not in that state at the time of the commission of the crime, and has not fled therefrom."

Jeremy Markovich in *Our State* magazine reported another twist to the case. The missing moonshine still that ignited the confrontation wasn't "missing" so much as "reclaimed." Bryson had originally stolen the still from a neighboring farmer, who came and took it back, unbeknownst to Bryson or Hall.

POPCORN SUTTON

A writer of penny-dreadful stories during the late 1800s bestowed on tall, handsome, battle-worn Lewis Redmond the title "King of the Moonshiners." The tales embellished Redmond's exploits into legends befitting moonshining royalty. At the end of the next century, the title was unofficially passed to a man whose overalls hung off his slumped, slim body. His scraggly beard obscured his chest, and his large eyes always carried a question or a challenge.

In 1949, Melvin "Popcorn" Sutton was born in Maggie Valley, North Carolina, and lived his life ranging between there and places across the line in Tennessee. He grew up playing the banjo with his mother, but liquor-making was the family business. As the foreword to his autobiography explained, he learned that "very few people were willing to put in the hard work necessary to build a good 'pot' or to make good liquor." Popcorn could do the hard work required to build the still, and he could make what others termed good liquor. "I have never sold a man or a woman a jar of likker that they didn't come back for some more," he wrote.

His photocopied autobiography, which sells now for hundreds of dollars online, detailed the making of liquor and the importance of stainless steel cook pots—one of his pots "helt" three hundred gallons. He disdained those who cooked in sheet metal pots. He warned of the dangers of being near so much stainless steel and copper in a lightning storm and described the difference in sweet mash (the first run) and sour mash (the second).

He readily taught those willing to learn the craft of making liquor and expressed his admiration for the big men who could carry a hundred-pound barrel with a couple hundred pounds of sugar in one load. He talked about working with an older husband and wife who cooked with wood and the effort of chopping that much wood. Personally, he preferred to use gas and kerosene in his larger, more modern—but equally illegal—operations.

Like lots of folks who grew up poor and making do in the mountains, Popcorn could modify everything from his 1964 Ford Galaxie to create a dust screen for eluding pursuers to altering an old electric coffee grinder from an A&P Grocery to grind his corn, rye and barley mash. He knew how to scout locations for stills, hidden from lawmen, that had good spring water

Popcorn Sutton, *on left*, at his still with J.B. Rader. *Courtesy of Neal Hutcheson and his book*, The Moonshiner Popcorn Sutton.

Popcorn Sutton. *Courtesy of Neal Hutcheson and his book*, The Moonshiner Popcorn Sutton.

and paths to get supplies in and product out. He said, "I've carried enough sugar that I have Dixie Crystals stamped on my right shoulder and on the other shoulder I've got Ball-Mason fruit jars stamped on it."

His technical skills and his attention to detail—like measuring how much liquor was produced by a run at different temperatures or at different times of the year or where to buy sugar or wheat bran in bulk—helped him make good liquor. But his marketing skills helped make him a legend.

He said he'd been tried twice on liquor charges—both times, he said, "Somebody ratted me out." He also knew he couldn't tell who turned him in. "You might get ideas, but you can never pinpoint it."

When he wasn't back in the woods working, Popcorn ran the Old Store, what he called his junk store, in Maggie Valley near the entrance to the Ghost Town in the Sky theme park. In a 2005 article, the Haywood County newspaper highlighted Popcorn's fame as a boost to Maggie Valley tourism. Stories about Popcorn recount how he got the only name he would answer to—in a fight with a barroom popcorn machine that wouldn't give him any popcorn or his money back. Reports say the popcorn machine lost, but Popcorn said it cost him seventy-five dollars.

He said that eventually his back wore out from carrying hundred-pound bags of sugar and the law was looking too closely at him, but the legend of Popcorn Sutton continued, told in newspaper and magazine stories, in documentaries, in photography books and in appearances at festivals around the region. He promoted restaurants, inns, other businesses, young musicians and people he liked in the Maggie Valley area.

He also worked with filmmaker Neal Hutcheson at North Carolina State University on a documentary in 2002, *This Is the Last Run of Likker I'll Ever Make*. Popcorn told Hutcheson that he wanted the film to be long so people would get their money's worth. Popcorn proved to be an able marketer and salesman to residents and tourists in Maggie Valley. Thanks to his efforts, the VHS tape sold well.

In 2007, to commemorate Popcorn's last batch, Hutcheson used that earlier footage and did additional filming to create *The Last One*, which won a regional Emmy and aired on PBS.

On March 13, 2008, Popcorn was arrested and jailed in Greeneville, Tennessee, for possessing illegal liquor there and in North Carolina. He had pledged in 2002, as part of his personal documentary about his last batch, that he was done making liquor. But in April 2007, at his home near Parrotsville, Tennessee, a fire erupted when his still blew up. That time, he received probation.

When federal ATF agents raided his home in March of the following year, they found three one-thousand-gallon-capacity stills and eight hundred gallons of liquor. The lawmen just couldn't turn a blind eye. In January, instead of the maximum of fifteen years, Popcorn was sentenced to eighteen months. On March 16, 2009, days before he was to report to prison, his wife of two years came home from running errands and found him sitting in his Ford Fairmont, dead of carbon monoxide poisoning. Popcorn was sixty-two years old.

About a year after Popcorn's death, Tennessee and South Carolina were among the southern states that began to legalize moonshine distilleries, although North Carolina didn't join the movement.

In 2021, filmmaker Neal Hutcheson published *The Moonshiner Popcorn Sutton* as a tribute to a complex man he'd gotten to know over several years—a storyteller, a craftsman, an entertainer and among the last of that particular breed of mountain men.

THE MURDER BALLADS

Born in the oral traditions of Ireland, Scotland and England and enriched in the protected hollows of the Southern Appalachian Mountains, ballads are a combination of life lessons and history, musical entertainment and warning. Some of them deal with love and yearning, but the most memorable deal with love gone wrong and tragic, murderous endings.

TOM DULA

The ballads were often collected by folklorists—academics, amateur historians and musicians who recorded or transcribed to paper the old story-songs. Some of this music spread far beyond the mountains, made popular by folk singers such as the Kingston Trio, who in 1958 recorded "Tom Dooley." The song sold 6 million copies and is often credited with launching the popularity of folk music that carried into the 1960s, but it started as the story of star-crossed North Carolina lovers Tom Dula and Laura Foster.

Even though the backdrop and the times are different, ill-fated love affairs today can still spark the same violence and headlines. Tom Dula had returned to Wilkes County at the end of the Civil War and took up life as a popular fiddle player, much requested at local gatherings around the area. He also took up a reputation as a ladies' man and was keeping regular company with at least two young women: Laura Foster and Ann Melton.

By some accounts, Laura Foster was a girl with an easy reputation. Or perhaps he contracted a venereal disease from someone else. In any event, he was threatening to kill whoever had given it to him.

According to the *New York Herald*, outsiders considered southern mountain people to be "ignorant, poor, and depraved," so it was little surprise to outsiders who commented on the case that these Wilkes County couples were running around contracting the pox and conceiving out of wedlock. "A state of immorality unexampled in the history of any country exists among these people, and such a general system of free lovism prevails, that it is 'a wise child that knows its father.'"

As the facts were later pieced together, on May 25, 1866, Laura was riding her father's horse and carrying a bundle of clothes when she encountered one of her friends, Betsey Scott. What passed between the two friends eventually became the subject of much legal dispute, but in the first trial, Betsey was allowed to testify that Laura said she was heading to a spot near the Bates place for a rendezvous with Tom Dula. Tom was supposed to arrive there by a different road, so they wouldn't be seen together.

On June 18, Laura's decomposing body was found "rudely buried in a laurel thicket" not far from where she was supposed to meet Tom. She had been stabbed once in the left side of her chest.

Tom Dula was arrested for murder. His other girlfriend, Ann Melton, was arrested as his accomplice before the fact, but the charges against her were dropped because Dula intervened on her behalf. He insisted that he was innocent and demanded his case be heard by a jury. His trial was moved to Statesville because local sentiment in Wilkes County didn't favor Tom.

At trial, the jury heard that he was "in the habit of criminal intercourse" with both Ann and Laura—nineteenth-century legalese for "fooling around." They also heard that Tom had spent time the weekend before Laura's death at Ann's house, that Ann had made convoluted arrangements to get some moonshine liquor to Tom and that he was seen near the Bates place on the day Laura died, carrying a mattock borrowed from his mother.

However, the clearest evidence linking Laura and Tom at the time she disappeared was Betsey Scott's testimony about her conversation with Laura. She reported that Laura was running away with Tom, and then Laura disappeared. The jury was left with the clear impression that Laura expected the start of an exciting new life when she was, in fact, riding a borrowed horse to her death.

The jury convicted Tom, and he appealed to the North Carolina Supreme Court. His lawyer argued that Betsey's testimony was hearsay, that she shouldn't have been allowed to repeat what Laura said when Laura wasn't there to be cross-examined. Betsey could tell the jury that Laura was riding her father's horse bareback, carrying a bundle of clothes and heading toward the Bates place because Betsey witnessed those actions, but Betsey couldn't repeat the conversation about where Tom was or that Laura expected to meet him.

The appellate court agreed that Betsey's hearsay testimony shouldn't have been heard. The chief justice, in the court's written opinion, said, "The case discloses a most horrible murder, and the public interest demands that the perpetrator of the crime should suffer death; but the public interest also demands that the prisoner, even if he be guilty, shall not be convicted, unless his guilt can be proved according to the law of the land."

At a new trial, a second jury again found Tom guilty, and he again appealed. Courts didn't waste much time in those days. His first appeal was heard in the January 1867 court term. It took only a year for Tom to have a second jury trial and for his appeal to be heard in the January 1868 term. This time, the appellate court upheld this conviction.

The ballad is based in fact—fact so solid that his two legal appeals are available online. Unlike the lyrics, though, Tom Dula did not initially hang his head and confess to killing Laura Foster. Instead, he fought through the court system before he faced the hangman two years after Laura's death.

Richard H. Underwood, a law professor at the University of Kentucky, published an entertaining and well-researched book, *CrimeSong*, exploring the real crimes behind murder ballads in the South. To Tom Dula's story, he brought his expertise on evidence law to dissect the legal appeals.

Murder ballads bear notable similarities to the confessional broadsides first published in early nineteenth-century England. As literacy rates increased and printing prices decreased, the broadsides became the original true crime podcasts, giving the public the gory details of trials, confessions and hangings, all for less than a penny. The key, though, was the confessional aspect. If the public was to learn anything from a tragic end on the gallows, the lesson was best delivered by the killer's own confession as to how he'd gone wrong and his warning to others about the inevitable consequences of an evil act.

On May 1, 1868, Tom Dula was hanged for murder, with an estimated three thousand people attending. Standing on the gallows constructed for the occasion at the Statesville depot, Dula made a textbook gallows confession, in the best tradition of such preparations for judgment in the

LAURA FOSTER

DIED MAY 28, 1866
MAY SHE REST IN PEACE

ON THE 28TH OF MAY, 1866, LAURA FOSTER, A BEAUTIFUL BUT FRAIL GIRL, WAS DECOYED FROM HER FATHER'S HOUSE AT GERMAN HILL IN CALDWELL COUNTY TO A PLACE IN WILKES COUNTY AND WAS MURDERED. TOM DULA (TOM DOOLEY) WAS LATER HANGED FOR HER MURDER. SHE WAS BURIED ON THE BANK OF THE YADKIN RIVER ON THE FARM OF JOHN WALTER WINKLER.

LAURA'S GRAVE IS ACROSS THE ROAD SURROUNDED BY THE WHITEWASHED LOCUST FENCE. THE LAND FOR THIS PARK IS PROVIDED BY JOHN CHRISTIAN BERNHARDT.

THIS HISTORICAL MARKER IS PROVIDED BY
WOODMEN OF THE WORLD LODGE 95
LENOIR, NORTH CAROLINA
1991

Above: Memorial for Laura Foster on Highway 268, detailing her murder in 1866. *Photo by Cathy Pickens.*

Left: Tom Dula's grave lies on private property on this road off Highway 268. *Photo by Cathy Pickens.*

Opposite: Laura Foster's grave site, located on private land across the road from her memorial and marked by a white fence. *Photo by Cathy Pickens.*

next life—one suitable for printing in a British-style broadside or turning into a southern murder ballad. He confessed to murdering Laura and removed his other lover from suspicion with the assurance, "I declare that I am the only person that had a hand in the murder of Laura Foster."

Frankie Silver

One of the most enduring and debated mountain murder stories is that of Frankie Silver. Is it because Frankie was the first woman sent to the gallows in North Carolina? That's the accepted story, although it's not true. She likely was closer to the tenth or fifteenth woman hanged in North Carolina, although records on local executions were not consolidated until the state took over the business of meting out justice in 1910.

Has the story endured because of doubts about whether she was the one who killed her husband? Did she take the blame for someone else in her family? Did she get so angry that she chopped her husband up and disposed of the bits? Or is it just hard to believe that a wife could be so afraid that she struck out at her much larger husband as he attacked her…and that she happened to land a tragically lucky blow? The story has persisted because those questions are so hard to answer.

Frankie's ballad never hit the pop charts as Tom Dula's did, and despite legend saying that she penned it herself and sang it from the gallows as a confession, she likely couldn't have. Frankie probably could not read or write. But a ballad telling her story was inevitably written and performed because, as noted by Muriel Earley Sheppard in her *Cabins in the Laurels*, it was "the most sensational murder case in the history of the Toe River Valley."

What the jury heard was that, on the night of December 22, 1831, Frankie took an axe—valued at six pence, according to the indictment—and murdered her husband in his sleep. On a snowy evening, after he did the hard work of chopping wood so Frankie could heat the house while he was gone on a hunting trip, he fell asleep in front of the fire in their one-room cabin, maybe after playing a bit with their baby.

Did Frankie kill him out of jealousy because he was going to disappear for a week or two, saying that he was hunting bear or deer but just as likely staying over with another woman? Or did she defend herself because he beat her when he got drunk?

At six feet tall, Charlie Silver was a nice-looking man known as the life of the party. Frankie was a year younger and described by her brother-in-law, Alfred Silver, as "a mighty likely little woman. She had charms, I never saw a smarter little woman."

Charlie Silver had gone that day to pick up the liquor for the Christmas holiday gathering. Charlie was not averse to drinking and liked a good party. But at trial, no one talked about whether he was a fun drunk, and among her family, there was plenty of talk that he could be mean and abusive. But at

Old Kona Baptist Church, the Silver family church in Mitchell County. *Photo by Cathy Pickens.*

that time, women were little more than property, so what did how he treated her have to do with a murder case?

Putting aside the arguments designed to defend or condemn, the evidence suggested that Frankie took an axe to her husband and killed him. The jury might have accepted the killing more easily than what she did next. Likely in a panic, she dismembered him and tried to burn him in the fireplace. As many a murderer can attest, a cabin fireplace isn't going to burn hot enough to dispose of the remains of a healthy six-foot man. She even tried to hide his head and torso outside the cabin. But soon, a suspicious neighbor started snooping around and found evidence of a bloody scene.

What happened to Charlie and his body left a trail not difficult to follow. But other questions remained: Had her family helped her dispose of the body? Wouldn't a mother and brother do that for a young woman in a panic? Had Frankie done it in premeditated anger and frustration? Or was it self-defense against a large, drunken husband?

Frankie; her mother, Barbara; and brother, Blackston Silver, were arrested on January 9, 1832, and moved to the jail in Morganton the next day. A week later, the charges against her family were dropped, leaving Frankie alone, awaiting trial.

Her two-day trial began on March 29, 1832, at the Burke County courthouse. At the time, women were allowed to testify in court, but defendants could not take the stand in their own defense. They were seen as biased in their own favor. Frankie's defense lawyer stuck with her family's contention that she had nothing to do with the death. He seemed confident they could win the day without putting on much of a case, that the state would have trouble convincing a jury she'd done it—probably because he knew that the notion of a small woman killing her strapping outdoorsman husband would seem physically unlikely. "Spousal abuse" would be a defense only for people far in the future and far away from a Toe River cabin.

Her claim of innocence might have been working for her—after some deliberation, the jury was reportedly hung nine to three in favor of acquittal. However, when the jury asked the judge if they could recall some witnesses for more questions, things took a bad turn for Frankie.

As Professor Underwood explained, North Carolina courts followed Rule 615, known as the Rule of Witnesses or the Rule of Exclusion, which allowed counsel or the judge to sequester or exclude witnesses from hearing the testimony of other witnesses during a trial. The rule was designed to prevent witnesses from making sure their stories agreed with what others said. The source of the rule may be the ancient tale of Susanna and the Elders, where Daniel saved Susanna, a woman wrongly accused of adultery by two jilted men. Adultery carried a death sentence, but Daniel intervened in her trial and kept the witnesses from hearing each other's testimony. Their falsehood became clear, and Susanna's life was saved. The story was omitted from the Protestant version of the Bible as apocryphal, but it still made sound legal sense.

Charlie Silver's grave is marked by three weathered stones and a newer marker that reads, "Charles Silver, Oct. 3, 1812–Dec. 22, 1831." *Photo by Cathy Pickens.*

During their deliberations, modern juries can ask to see pieces of evidence, have points of law explained or have portions of testimony re-read. But Frankie's jury had already begun discussing the case. And the witnesses had been hanging around the courthouse together, with no prohibitions against talking to each other. The judge should have denied this past-the-twelfth-hour request by the jurors to hear new testimony, but he allowed it. The jury returned later that day with a unanimous verdict: guilty.

As Frankie's case was appealed and her execution date drew near, the community sentiment in favor of pardoning her grew. Even members of the jury signed the petition to the governor. For whatever reasons, the new governor refused to intervene. With no other hope, her father and two accomplices engineered a jail break, but her freedom lasted only eight days. Frankie was hanged in Morganton, in what is now Mitchell County, on July 12, 1833.

The lingering questions have kept the story alive for almost two hundred years because, at such a distance, the answer can never be clear. Through the lens of a society that puts a name to and penalizes domestic violence, can we understand a patriarchal mountain society? Or a society where families, to this day, still live close together in the same community?

If it was self-defense, why did her lawyer not build that case? Did he want to avoid difficult questions about the family's involvement in disposing of the body? Or their help in her escape before her trial? Or did he simply believe that a jury wouldn't convict a woman? The double standard operated in southern courts, then as now, in seeing women as the weaker and less violent gender.

Author Perry Deane Young shared a view of the case from a long line of noteworthy North Carolina legal figures. Senator Sam Ervin Jr. heard the story from his father, who heard it from attorney Burgess Sidney Gaither, who served as law clerk during Frankie's trial—a long line of good historians:

> [Gaither] *was wont to assert that she would not have been convicted if the truth had been disclosed on the trial....Silver mistreated his wife and she killed him in protection of herself. And Colonel Gaither always entertained the opinion that if the defense had admitted the killing the jury would have found her act justified and would have acquitted her. The defense, however, was a denial that the hand of Frankie Silver struck the fatal blow and* [there] *being evidence of her guilt, the jury following the instinct of the sleuth which lurks in every human mind, promptly convicted her of willful murder.*

Wayne Silver, a Silver family historian and retired businessman who is often interviewed about the case, finds Frankie killing her husband in a jealous rage unlikely. More likely, Frankie picked up an axe to defend herself and her child from a large, angry man who'd had too much to drink. In a *Blue Ridge* magazine interview, Silver said, "I will never believe it was premeditated murder and few in my family have ever believed it. In fact, it was more of an accident than anything else."

Any story almost two hundred years old will gather embellishments and misinformation. Some parts of the story were too unimportant, too painful or too risky to record at the time. And southern storytellers are not known for letting facts get in the way of a good story. For those interested in the details around Frankie's real story, Perry Deane Young's thoroughly researched *The Untold Story of Frankie Silver* includes copies of original documents and sources for the different versions of the story. Young grew up hearing accounts of what happened just over the mountain from where he lived, and his kinfolk likely sold liquor to Charlie Silver, back in the day.

OMIE WISE

While murder ballads were nurtured and shared over the years within the mountains, not all the songs and stories originated there. After all, settlers from the ballad-rich Scotch-Irish traditions also settled elsewhere in North Carolina. Omie Wise lived in Randleman, south of Greensboro, and not in Western North Carolina. But her short life and the tragedy of her death became a classic North Carolina murder ballad popularized by Doc Watson, one of Western North Carolina's most famous folk singers, as well as Bob Dylan and others.

Doc Watson was a flat-pick guitarist and singer of traditional songs. Others called it "folk music." In the way African American cuisine is often called "soul food"—although most southerners, especially Black southerners, just call it food—most who grow up clog dancing and playing and listening to acoustic bluegrass and mountain music just call it "music."

Born in Stoney Fork, in the Deep Gap area of the mountains, Doc Watson was left blind after an eye infection as an infant. One of nine children in a farm family, Watson credits his father with helping him with his music and with figuring out how to live his life. His 2012 *New York Times* obituary quoted a 1979 *Frets* magazine interview: "I would not have been worth the salt that went in my bread if my dad hadn't put me at the end of a crosscut saw to show me that there was not a reason in the world that I couldn't pull my weight and help to do my part in some of the hard work."

His dad led the singing at their Baptist church and saw that Doc Watson got a guitar. Doc grew up immersed in mountain culture, surrounded by church music, shape-note singing and ballads of love and loss. He listened to other artists and developed his own style. For listeners around the country first discovering "folk" music, Watson delivered the genuine article. He brought music from the mountains to a wider audience of country, bluegrass and folk music fans.

The ballads he learned from his mother and from others had an even longer history. The story told in Omie Wise's ballad echoes the song "The Banks of the Ohio" that Doc Watson sang with bluegrass legend Bill Monroe. Singer Olivia Newton-John later brought it to a worldwide audience. The haunting opening line, "I asked my love to take a walk," moves from a lover's tryst to murder and regret, a common storyline in the mountain murder ballads and the older ones brought over on sailing ships in the 1700s.

As with any oral tradition passed down through generations, the versions of Omie's story vary in the details but unfold along sad and predictable paths. As researchers tried to piece together the story that prompted Omie's ballad, the details got even more confusing.

Most accounts of Omie Wise's life draw from the version written by Braxton Craven, who grew up only a few hundred yards from the Deep River south of Randleman. His two-part account, written less than fifty years after her murder, appeared in the January and February 1851 edition of *Evergreen* and is the touchstone for the ballads and stories that followed.

Craven reported that the orphaned Naomi Wise was taken in by a farm family in Randolph County. As a teenager, she met Jonathan Lewis, a young man who didn't mind dawdling with the girl for entertainment but who intended to marry his employer's sister, a girl with more money and more position in the community.

Sometime in April 1807, when his relationship with Omie became inconvenient, she disappeared. Searchers found her body in the Deep River. Accounts said that she was pregnant. Accounts also said that Jonathan took Omie on horseback and rode with her into the river. He strangled her and then pulled her skirts over her head, tied a knot at the hem and held her underwater. A nearby resident said that she heard screams.

Those who knew Omie knew to go looking for Jonathan Lewis. Reports said that when they captured Jonathan and hauled him to the riverside to confront the body, he smoothed her hair from her face and seemed notably unfazed by the sight of the dead woman.

Craven collected the facts from old-timers who recalled the tragedy. He also invented dialogue that no one but the killer could have known; given the unlikely physical maneuvering described in the drowning, much of Craven's account likely was an exercise in creative license.

The public record shows that on March 30, 1807, the grand jury indicted Jonathan Lewis for murder. He was turned over to the Randolph County Jail on April 8 and his trial set for October 26. Interestingly, the ballads traditionally give 1808 as the year of her death.

After the sheriff alerted the magistrates of plans for a jailbreak, militiamen were detailed to guard the jail. Despite the precautions, Jonathan escaped and stayed on the run for several years. The accounts vary about how long. In an odd twist, the sheriff was charged with aiding the escape. The charges were dropped only after he helped bring Jonathan back to North Carolina. The four other men convicted in the escape were released when the governor granted clemency.

At this point, Craven's account of the story and its later retelling in a 1944 book, published by the Rotary Club of Randleman commemorating the town's history, both veer from the official documents. The more colorful accounts have Jonathan Lewis setting up a life for himself in Kentucky or elsewhere. In fact, he was recaptured in 1811 and tried in 1812. And his charges in the court documents come as a surprise to those looking for resolution in the dramatic story of Omie Wise: he stood trial and was convicted for "breaking jail." He was found not guilty of helping another prisoner escape—and he was never tried for the murder of Naomi Wise at all.

Omie Wise's story holds other surprises. Another researcher, Eleanor R. Long-Wingus, found evidence that Omie Wise wasn't a susceptible young virgin but rather an older woman who'd already had children out of wedlock. Under the mores of that time, Omie would not have expected marriage, although perhaps she was demanding funds to support the child, known as a bastardy bond.

Looking past the romantic fable to the facts, it is easy to imagine a woman who already had children and worked a menial job. None too shy about enjoying "carnal knowledge" outside the bonds of matrimony, she could find herself longing for the attentions of a better class of man. Jonathan apparently worked as a secretary or clerk. He had a position in the community. Clearly it was wishful thinking on Omie's part, but she could dream, couldn't she? Maybe Jonathan would settle down with her, provide a good life for her and his baby.

Sure, she told people about the pregnancy, although the official accounts at the time don't state that she was pregnant when she died. Had she concocted a tale to trap Jonathan into a marriage proposal? Sure, a woman can fantasize about a better life than the one she is living. But as too often happens, then and now, a pregnant woman is at risk of murder from her intimate partner during and soon after a pregnancy—today, she's twice as likely to die of murder during that period than from any other cause.

Comparing reality with the poignant ballad leads back to a basic tale. Omie Wise was a real woman, and she was murdered. The man who murdered her was, by consistent accounts, in a better position than she was financially and socially. He tried to hide his deed. The reality of Omie's life was different from the tales told and sung, but as folklore writer Robert Roote characterized her story, "Where the age-old tales of deception are vague and impersonal, Naomi's localized tragedy is real. Naomi Wise *is* North Carolina's 'Murdered Girl' in the ballad tradition."

OMA HICKS

The ballad of the Big Bend killings didn't become as widely popular as other ballads, perhaps because of the isolation of the area, perhaps because the lessons were harder to draw. In this case, rather than being a susceptible innocent, the woman likely instigated the murders.

Did Oma Hicks know that a dalliance would lead to her husband's death? Did she spur the other men involved into forming a vigilante posse just to get rid of him?

Oma grew up in the Big Bend section of North Carolina, a remote, isolated area marked by a bend in the Pigeon River close to the border with Tennessee. No matter the law elsewhere in the country, the principal business of the families in Big Bend was bootlegging. When she was eighteen, she married thirty-eight-year-old Ben Naillon, a widower who'd grown up over in Tennessee and had done some traveling to Utah and Montana for his work as an animal driver or teamster. The couple moved to the Candler community, a few miles from Asheville.

Two years into their marriage, Ben up and disappeared. Had he taken off out west again? Or, as was later rumored, had Oma and her family—or maybe one of Oma's many admirers—made sure he disappeared? No word was heard from Ben after 1916, and his body was never found.

In these deep mountains, families handled their own matters. They'd also lived for generations together, in the kind of isolation than can lead to feuds that last so long the feuders forget what they were fighting over.

Sometime before 1930, Oma was back in Big Bend and married to Scott Brown. Oma and Scott worked in the community's chief industry: moonshining. Oma also continued, apparently, to attract and keep company with several young men, men her husband would also have known. After all, it was a close-knit community.

In August 1930, Scott and Mims White worked together at a second job at a sawmill a two-day walk from Big Bend. They were headed home at week's end, and after making the last steep climb to the ridge, they stopped for a break on the "resting log." As they looked out over valley, Oma came walking up the trail with Vester Brown. In the kind of tangled skein of relationships that can happen in an isolated area, Vester had recently been released from a prison term for murdering Oma's father in 1915.

The resting log wasn't just for resting tired legs after a long climb uphill. The lovely views and the isolation made it a nice spot for lovers. The story later told was that Scott confronted Vester. As the three men "got into it," Oma ran downhill to get help, to where she knew other men were finishing up a run of liquor on the still. Frank McGaha and Varnell Gates, Vester's half brother, ran up to the scene of the scuffle between Scott and Vester.

Scott Brown and Mims White were never seen alive again. Their families searched and asked questions, but no one was talking, except in whispers. And so things might have stood, except that federal agents started raiding stills and arresting moonshiners, including Vester, Varnell, Frank and even Oma.

Not surprisingly, when Oma was arrested and transported to the Buncombe County Jail, the newspapers revived the seventeen-year-old story about her first husband's disappearance. The *Asheville Citizen-Times* mistakenly reported Ben Naillon's name as Parker Naylor, but the implications were clear that something was askew with Oma and her unfortunate husbands.

Vacationing detective J.J. O'Malley came to the area to escape the late winter Chicago cold and heard the story of the two missing men. Like a plot twist in a vintage detective story, the out-of-towner took a busman's holiday and helped interrogate the jailed moonshiners. Eventually, their stories began to unravel.

O'Malley later told the newspaper that he spent time talking to people in Haywood County, in the Big Bend and Cataloochee sections, learning what he could about Oma, the woman who'd returned home to Big Bend after her first husband vanished from their marital home near Candler.

In April, after the visiting detective and local investigators gathered statements and leads from witnesses, they climbed the mountain to see where Scott Brown and Mims White were last seen. They uncovered their remains in the hole created by a giant tree uprooted in a storm. Scott had been shot in the head; Mims's skull was cracked into fragments.

Those who'd killed Scott and Mims, presumably to protect Oma from her husband's anger, had also come up with a plan to throw suspicion on Carl Miller, another man Scott suspected of a dalliance with his wife. They tossed papers bearing Miller's name into the makeshift grave. Miller was arrested and questioned but later released.

The Big Bend moonshiner trials took place a year too early for the 1932 opening of the Haywood County Courthouse. *Courtesy of Abe Ezekowitz via Wikimedia Commons.*

On July 23, 1931, Varnell, Vester and Frank pleaded guilty to the second-degree murder of Scott Brown; Varnell also pleaded guilty to Mims White's murder. At the same hearing in Waynesville, Oma Hicks Brown pleaded not guilty. The men maintained that Oma played no part in the murders, so the court accepted her not guilty plea and didn't proceed against her for the murder. She was, however, sentenced to a year in the Haywood County Jail for moonshining.

As noted in her well-researched and well-told tales of Western North Carolina, *Murder in the Mountains*, Nadia Dean noted that, a year later, Oma married Carl Miller—the man the killers tried to frame—and the two lived quietly until he died in 1960. He was seventy-three. Oma Hicks Naillon Brown Miller lived fourteen more years, to age seventy-seven, and was buried in Waynesville.

THE ASHEVILLE CASES

HELEN CLEVENGER

The death of slender, statuesque nineteen-year-old Helen Clevenger proved to be a double tragedy. On July 17, 1936, the college student from New York was found dead in room 224 of Asheville's Battery Park Hotel. Some guests heard screams from the direction of her room at about one o'clock in the morning, but no one had reason to check on her until her uncle came to wake her the next morning.

Helen had finished her freshman year at New York University, and the Staten Island native was enjoying her first visit to the South. Her bachelor uncle, Professor W.L. Clevenger, taught animal husbandry at North Carolina State College and provided advice to dairy farmers across the state as an extension agent. The professor wanted to inspire his bright niece to consider pursuing a demanding academic program such medicine or science. The night before, they had dinner with friends of his, and then Helen turned in about 10:30 p.m. to write in her journal and perhaps send some postcards, a nightly ritual for the young writer who wanted to capture the details of her summer adventure.

Later that evening, a thunderstorm ripped across Asheville, thunder booming off the surrounding mountains in a way that must be experienced to be believed. A guest heard what sounded like a gunshot and summoned house detective Daniel Gaddy—sometimes referred to as the night watchman—to the second floor. He saw nothing suspicious and figured that the storm was the most likely explanation.

Left: Vintage postcard of downtown Asheville, circa 1930. *Courtesy Durwood Barbour Collection of North Carolina Postcards, UNC, and W.M. Cline Company.*

Opposite: Battery Park Hotel at corner of Brattle Square and O'Henry. *Courtesy of Warren LeMay via flickr.com.*

The next morning, Professor Clevenger knocked several times on Helen's door. She didn't answer, and he heard no sounds inside her room. The night before, he'd arranged a wakeup call with the front desk. This was a working trip for him, and they had plans for an early breakfast. The doorknob turned when he tried it, and he found Helen lying on the floor, her face badly beaten and her green silk pajamas covered in blood.

The Battery Park Hotel, which opened in 1924, sat on the site of the original Battery Park Hotel, built in 1886—which, in turn, sat on the site of a military battery left from the Civil War. The original hotel had boasted electric lights and the first electric elevator in the South, but it had fallen into disrepair. Edwin Grove, who also built Asheville's Grove Park Inn, erected the new Battery Park. The twelve-story hotel—and the cool summer climate of Asheville—attracted tourists and celebrities. The city prospered during the 1920s, but the Depression years were not easy.

During their investigation, the police detained a German violinist simply because he'd brought his fiancée to the hotel for dinner the night of the murder. They also questioned sixty hotel employees and held Professor Clevenger, house detective Gaddy and two Black male employees in jail for additional questioning.

Police had only two pieces of evidence. One piece was eyewitness testimony about a man running along the porch on the hotel's second floor that night. A bellhop in the lobby also saw a man run out of a stairwell and through the screen door to the second-floor porch. A Blue Bird taxi driver pulled up to the hotel in time to see a man run toward the balcony railing. Witnesses said he "vaulted" over the balustrade and landed beside the entrance to the basement barbershop. He turned right onto O'Henry Avenue and ran alongside the hotel. They described what they thought was a lanky white man of average height and weight—less than six feet, about

160 or 170 pounds. The second piece of evidence was a .32-caliber casing found on the floor near Helen's body.

The scant evidence didn't mean authorities weren't searching for leads. Sheriff Laurence Brown mailed typed letters, dated July 30, to officials in other cities asking for information about those involved in the Asheville case. According to author Anne Chesky Smith's research, one letter asked the chief of New York's homicide squad to have someone interview Helen's parents and her friends at New York University. The sheriff included the

Clevengers' home address on Staten Island and Mr. Clevenger's work address at the federal Food and Drug Administration office. In particular, the sheriff wanted to know if Helen had a gun with her on her trip and if anything about her father's work "might make vindictive enemies."

Three weeks after Helen's death, despite the apparent zeal and thoroughness in looking at suspects, no one was under arrest. On August 7, the New York Police Department sent two homicide detectives to Asheville to lend their big-city expertise. The local papers didn't make big news of the city detectives' arrival, but the New York papers did.

Martin Moore, a twenty-two-year-old bellhop at the hotel, attracted police attention when they learned he owned a .32 pistol, the same caliber as the gun that killed Helen. Moore admitted he owned the .32. He'd recently loaned it to Lem Roddy, one of his workmates who lived down the street from him. He pointed police to the rafter under the porch of his house where he'd stowed it when Roddy returned it.

When the NYPD crime lab examined the gun, they found blood and "two little blonde hairs" similar to Helen's face hairs on the weapon—a forensic hair comparison that likely would not stand up in court today.

The second tragedy from that July night was the quick prosecution and execution of Martin Moore. Given facts later made public, his assertion that he'd been forced into a false confession was more than plausible. A young Black man too close to the scene of a brutal murder and authorities desperate to close a case in a city that relied on tourists meant that some wanted a quick solution by any means. Justice—or at least the appearance of it—was swift.

Moore allegedly confessed twice. The first time, he confessed to the New York detectives. Moore later said he only confessed after being coerced by one detective and beaten with a rubber hose "by a fat man from New York," apparently referring to Detective John J. Quinn Jr. Moore later said that a detective told him if he'd tell them what happened, he wouldn't let them beat him anymore. The second confession he reportedly made to a psychiatrist.

New York police commissioner Lewis Joseph Valentine congratulated the two detectives when they returned to New York and told the newspapers, "It was a wonderful piece of detective work. Good, hard work of this type should be an example to the entire force."

A letter to the editor of the Black-owned *New York Amsterdam* newspaper was sarcastic rather than complimentary: "I have just read that the confession, according to Moore, was obtained in the usual New York manner by a liberal application of rubber hose. What a wonderful piece of detective work!"

A U.S. Supreme Court decision in *Brown v. Mississippi* had held that a conviction using a confession coerced with force couldn't be upheld—a decision handed down five months before Helen's murder. But that didn't help Moore.

New York detective John Quinn Jr. died in 1939 at age thirty-one, after a long illness. According to the headline on his *New York Times* obituary, Quinn "helped solve sensational killings of last few years; aided in Titterton Case; praised by Commissioner for trapping girl's murderer in North Carolina."

JUST BEFORE QUINN WAS sent to Asheville in July 1936, he had helped solve the notorious New York City rape-murder of writer Nancy Titterton, the wife of an NBC radio executive. In 1928, while she worked at the publishing company Doubleday, Doran, Nancy proposed a mystery book-of-the-month club, the first of what soon became a popular service with mystery-reading fans like herself. Quinn was one of a legion of detectives assigned to the case because of the prominence of Nancy Titterton among the New York literati.

On Good Friday, she was home in her Beekman Place apartment working on her first novel. Evidence said that she likely let her killer into the apartment. She was attacked in her bedroom and dumped in the bathtub. Her fountain pen was found on her pillow. The killer had bound her and then cut off the binding and taken the cord with him—but not all of it. Under Nancy's body, police found a thirteen-inch piece of cord.

In this case, investigators relied on the forensic expertise of Dr. Alexander O. Gettler, a toxicologist for the New York City Medical Examiner's Office and also quite adept with a microscope. The officers delivered to Dr. Gettler's lab at Bellevue Hospital the cord, the linens from her bed and other physical evidence. Gettler found on the bed linens a single hair, which he identified as horsehair used in stuffing furniture cushions. The hair was too heavy, reasoned lead detective John Lyons, to blow into the bedroom from where a newly reupholstered love seat was located.

Quinn was credited in his obituary with tracing the source of the cord. After canvassing cord-makers in the region, police identified the manufacturer, who said that the cheap cord was used in making venetian blinds. They learned that the manufacturer had shipped a roll of that cording to the upholstery shop the Tittertons used.

The day before the murder, two delivery drivers had picked up a loveseat at the Tittertons' apartment to be reupholstered. The men from the shop were returning the sofa the next afternoon when they found Nancy dead.

The single horsehair from the sofa stuffing had no reason for being in the Tittertons' bedroom, and the cord had no reason for being underneath her body, unless it was left by the killer. That focused the detectives on the upholstery shop and on one of the deliverymen, Johnny Fiorenza, who had a police record.

After a session of the famous "third degree," Fiorenza admitted he'd returned to the apartment the morning after they picked up the sofa. He'd become fascinated by Nancy's charm and poise when he first saw her. She recognized him and opened the door. Nancy Titterton fought off his advances, and he killed her. Later that afternoon, he and his boss returned to deliver the small sofa and "found" Nancy. Reports of the case don't indicate whether Quinn had his rubber hose in the interrogation room in this case.

BACK IN ASHEVILLE, MARTIN Moore confessed that he entered the Battery Park room looking for cash and startled Helen while she was writing in her journal. He shot her and ran from the room. But his family insisted that he was at a birthday party that night and couldn't have been prowling around looking for empty rooms and things to steal at the hotel.

In August, the jury deliberated only an hour and convicted him, even though the shot he described didn't explain the screams or Helen's battered face or an eyewitness description of a different man seen running away.

While Moore sat in North Carolina's Central prison, he told an official, "If Roddy would only tell the truth….It just goes to show you can't rely on a friend." He also reportedly wrote to a brother of his co-worker and friend Lem Roddy, begging him to tell the truth—that Roddy was the one who had the gun that night.

Martin Moore was executed five months after his conviction, on December 11, 1936.

Local authorities hadn't focused solely on Moore. They had other suspects, including the son of a prominent man in Asheville. Newspapers in Atlanta and elsewhere reported accounts that the killer was the hotel manager's son or lived at the hotel. Although the leads were not widely publicized at the time, the sheriff didn't ignore them. During his July 30 letter-writing campaign, he wrote to the police chief in Winchester, Virginia, asking whether the suspect was in Winchester when the murder occurred and if he had "a reputation there for women, whiskey, etc." Any response to that or other inquiries was not part of the case's written record.

Three months after her murder, the Clevengers sued the Battery Park Hotel owners and manager for wrongful death, a civil court action alleging that their gross negligence led to the murder. Proving gross negligence requires willful, wanton or reckless conduct by the defendants and opens the possibility of a jury award for punitive damages. The family agreed to settle the suit for $6,000 (about $120,000 today).

The Battery Park Hotel closed as a hotel in 1972. The building was added to the National Register of Historic Places in 1979 and later converted into apartments.

For more details on Helen, her family and Asheville at the time of her death, Anne Chesky Smith's detailed research into original records—including the letters and papers of Sheriff Laurence Brown now maintained at the Swannanoa Valley Museum and History Center in Black Mountain—offers interesting reading in her book, *Murder at Asheville's Battery Park Hotel*.

WILL HARRIS SHOOTING SPREE AND THOMAS WOLFE

A man called Will Harris (although his true identity was uncertain) traveled from Charlotte to Asheville in November 1906 and apparently didn't take long to find his way into a woman's bed—a married woman, no less, which didn't sit right with her husband. When the husband discovered the two, Harris fired his rifle at the cuckolded husband, who took off running for the police.

Harris didn't hit the husband, but he killed the constable and wounded the captain who responded to the summons. He then ran down Eagle Street, not far from Pack Square, shooting at random passersby. He killed five victims, wounded others and went on the run, hiding from searchers for two days before he was surrounded in a barn near Fletcher, south of Asheville. A posse of a reported one hundred men rode from Asheville and surrounded the barn. Harris returned fire until he ran out of ammunition, and then he was shot and killed.

Novelist Thomas Wolfe grew up in Asheville, which he called "Altamont" in his first novel, *Look Homeward, Angel*. Wolfe, the youngest in a large family, would have been six years old at the time Will Harris came to town. Wolfe lived with his mother at her boardinghouse at 48 Spruce Street, now a National Historic Landmark. The house stood only a few blocks from the scene of the shootings.

Such a dramatic story left its mark on Wolfe's imagination, as it marked the memory of most who lived in Asheville. In September 1937, only a

The Asheville boardinghouse where Thomas Wolfe spent part of his childhood, now a National Historic Landmark. *Courtesy of Abe Ezekowitz via Wikimedia Commons.*

year before his own early death, Wolfe published a short story based on the events, "The Child by Tiger," in the *Saturday Evening Post.*

The narrator in the story looks back in time: "The years passed, and all of us were given unto time. We went our ways. But often they would turn and come again, these faces and these voices of the past, and burn there in my memory....Then I would hear the furious bell, the crowd a-clamor and the baying of the dogs, and feel the shadow coming that would never disappear."

Wolfe's fictional account followed fairly closely what happened the day of the shootings, although he added a few extra murders. In his story, the posse searching for the fictional killer Dick Prosser is angry and violent. But according to Steve Haste, writing about true crime stories used in fiction and drama, contemporary news reports about the hunt for Will Harris said that the multiracial Asheville posse was calm and determined in its mission, not angry or violent.

In much of Wolfe's work, he relied heavily on the Asheville he remembered. The Will Harris story, as Wolfe used it in "The Child by Tiger," reappeared with few changes in Wolfe's novel *The Web and the Rock,* published a year after his death.

THE BILTMORE LIBRARY

Comedian Tim Conway came to Asheville to play a private eye in a movie. He didn't expect to help uncover a theft of valuable books. Some who'd never visited Western North Carolina became acquainted with its most iconic residence, Biltmore, watching *The Private Eyes*, a 1980 movie starring Tim Conway and Don Knotts. During the filming, a real mystery came to light.

George Vanderbilt, grandson of Cornelius Vanderbilt, fell in love with the North Carolina mountains around Asheville during a visit in 1888. He set about the task of building a home, but this was to be no ordinary country estate. The 250 rooms—with some secret rooms and hidden doors—filled more than 4 acres of interior space and originally sat on 125,000 acres of land. For all the robber baron–era lavishness of his building, Vanderbilt also brought forward-thinking forest conservation methods to the United States.

Much of the virgin forest in Western North Carolina had been logged to supply lumber for the nation's building boom and was depleted by subsistence farming. Vanderbilt hired Frederick Law Olmsted, who designed New York's Central Park, to oversee the design of his grounds and reforest the land in order to replenish wildlife and improve the waterways.

While at the same time traveling between Asheville and Chicago as he designed the landscaping for that city's 1893 World's Fair, Olmsted developed his plans for Biltmore and hired Gifford Pinchot to create the nation's first managed forest. Pinchot later became the first to lead the U.S. Forest Service. In 1914, Edith Vanderbilt sold eighty-seven thousand acres of the estate to the federal government at five dollars per acre to create what became the first national forest, Pisgah.

With the nation's largest privately held residence, the Vanderbilt legacy in the Asheville area is hard to ignore. But Vanderbilt didn't just acquire

A 1921 postcard showing the Biltmore Estate and its surrounding forest. *Courtesy of Durwood Barbour Collection of North Carolina Postcards, UNC.*

Above: A 1905 postcard showing a logging operation in Western North Carolina. *Courtesy of Durwood Barbour Collection of North Carolina Postcards, UNC.*

Opposite: A missing copy of Samuel Johnson's *Dictionary of the English Language* alerted authorities to the theft of rare volumes. *Courtesy of publicdomainreview.org.*

land and create massive architecture. He filled the house with artworks and valuable pieces of history from around the world.

The Private Eyes movie spoofed the Sherlock Holmes mysteries, using the Biltmore home as the backdrop. During idle moments while the crew occupied the house for the filming, Tim Conway was drawn to the massive library. George Vanderbilt was no casual collector of books solely for their bindings. He was insatiably curious and an avid reader, credited with reading an average of eighty-one books per year.

Given the actor's interest, a staff member offered to show him the 1756 edition of Samuel Johnson's *A Dictionary of the English Language*, only to find that the $7,500 two-volume set was missing.

The staff called authorities, and in looking through the library, they found other treasures missing, among them Edmund Spenser's *The Faerie Queene* and an 1887 edition of Eadweard Muybridge's *Animal Locomotion*, a series of photographs demonstrating the first stop-action study of the movement of a running horse, valued at $100,000. The library was also missing rare volumes by Lewis Carroll, the Brothers Grimm, *The Book of Common Prayer* and a portfolio of Goya etchings.

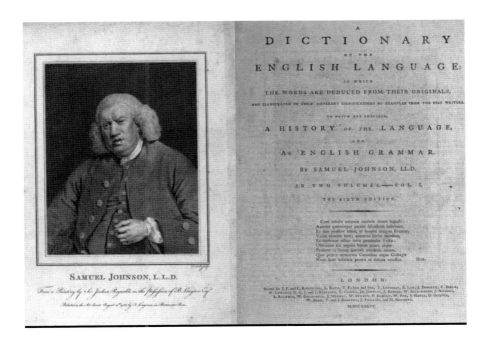

A full inventory revealed a theft beyond what the staff imagined. The library housed 10,000 of the collection's 24,000 volumes, and 234 of its rare items were missing.

The FBI's investigation discovered the thief very close to home. Rustem Levni Turkseven worked as a nighttime security guard at the estate for about a year and a half, starting in 1979. By day, though, Turkseven was Harvard-educated Robert Livingston Matters.

Matters owned Plane Tree Book Store at 12½ Wall Street in downtown Asheville and repaired antique book bindings. This wasn't the first time Matters had come under scrutiny for light fingers around valuable books. Other libraries suspected him of pilfering from their collections, but few wanted to publicize the thefts for fear of damage to their reputations or of calling attention to their vulnerable security.

For the Biltmore thefts, Matters pleaded guilty in 1981 to four counts of interstate transportation of stolen materials and was sentenced to five years. The FBI, with help from an antiquarian booksellers association, took two years but did recover all the missing volumes from across the United States, Canada and Europe and returned them to Biltmore's library.

William A.V. Cecil, George Vanderbilt's grandson and the operator of the Biltmore Estate, told the *Asheville Citizen-Times* that focusing on the appraised value of the books couldn't tell the whole story. Because the books had been acquired by and associated with the Vanderbilts, "they'd be impossible to replace."

NOTE: The Antiquarian Booksellers' Association of America maintains a Theft and Fraud website (https://www.abaa.org/security) for reporting missing or stolen books and suspected fraud. According to the site, "ABAA members have worked with local law enforcement agencies, FBI, Homeland Security and Interpol in efforts against biblio-crime." The International League of Antiquarian Booksellers (ILAB) maintains a missing book register (https://missingbooksregister.org).

HEADLINE CASES

When local cases make national and international news, the headlines tend to highlight what those outside the region would find unusual or quirky or odd. In the southern mountain regions, the stories often focus on the mystique of odd characters not quite right in the head, wild environs that easily hide secrets and stories that wouldn't happen somewhere else—or at least not in quite the same way.

MISSING HIKERS AND A SERIAL KILLER

For those who love to hike on ridges or along noisy streams, who study biodiverse plant life and feast on vistas, the mountains aren't mysterious or odd. The trails are peaceful and soul-filling. Irene Bryant, eighty-four, and her husband, John "Jack" Bryant, almost eighty, loved being in the woods and hiking the mountains together. Jack had hiked the length of the Appalachian Trail, and they always spent time on distant trails during their frequent trips abroad.

Married for fifty-eight years, the couple started taking hiking dates together when they first met. Irene was a large-animal vet and Jack an engineer who later attended law school. They'd lived in Montana and Upstate New York but chose Horse Shoe, North Carolina, as the place to retire. Between Hendersonville and the boundary of the Pisgah National Forest, Horse Shoe offered them a less wintry climate and an abundance of hiking trails.

Sign for Pisgah National Forest. *Photo by Cathy Pickens.*

On October 21, 2007, the couple laced up their walking shoes and headed out for their weekly hike in the Pisgah National Forest to enjoy one of the peak days for fall color. They chose the Pink Beds Trail off Highway 276 between Brevard and Waynesville, an easy five-mile loop through stands of trees and a forest bog.

The couple never returned from that October hike. Searchers located their Ford Escape parked on Yellow Gap Road near the Pink Beds Trail. Irene's body was just yards away, covered with leaves. She'd been struck in the head.

They didn't find Jack, and investigators had to wonder if he'd been responsible for Irene's death. But a few days after the couple went hiking, someone who wasn't Jack, wearing a yellow raincoat with the hood over his head, used the couple's ATM card at a Ducktown, Tennessee bank, about three hours west of the Bryants' home. Now investigators were looking for Jack's body and for the shadowy figure on the ATM video.

After Irene's murder and Jack's disappearance, at least three months passed before investigators could connect the scene at Pink Beds with later victims in Florida and Georgia and understand just how convoluted tracking this killer would be. He'd already made mistakes. He just hadn't made enough mistakes for investigators to identify him.

At least three cases were unfolding in three different states and on different timelines. What happened to the Bryants marked the beginning of the trail for investigators, but the track wasn't clear until the last attack, when the scattered threads could be pulled together.

The first thread was finding Irene Bryant's body and Jack missing on November 9, 2007. The second came in Florida on Saturday, December 1, more than four hundred miles from the Pisgah hiking trail. Cheryl Dunlap, a nurse at Florida State University, disappeared from the Leon Sinks area in the Apalachicola National Forest outside Tallahassee. Her coworkers reported her missing when she didn't come to work, and her car was found abandoned on the side of the Crawfordville Highway only a few miles from the park area.

Two weeks later, a hunter found a decapitated body in the forest. DNA confirmed the remains as forty-six-year-old Cheryl Dunlap.

A little over two weeks after that discovery, in yet another state, the third thread appeared. Twenty-four-year-old Meredith Emerson from Buford, Georgia, went hiking with her dog, Ella, in North Georgia's Vogel State Park to celebrate New Year's Day. Meredith was an avid hiker and loved the Coosa Backcountry Trail, a spur leading to the Appalachian Trail and popular with day-hikers from the Atlanta area. When Meredith wasn't home by the next day, her friends started searching for her.

The events of that January snowballed, leading to the capture of the man responsible for all three attacks—on the Bryants, Cheryl Dunlap and Meredith Emerson—as well as perhaps others. Unfortunately, the leads didn't come together quickly enough for investigators and families.

On the day before anyone knew that Meredith was missing, a former law enforcement officer, Sean Blankenship, was hiking the Coosa Trail to Blood Mountain and saw things that worried him. A scruffy, toothless man wearing a police baton in a sheath walked near an attractive, athletic young woman. At first, he thought it might be a father and daughter out for a hike.

Later, though, he came across a spot where the leaves and earth had been churned up, as if someone or something had been in a fight. A water bottle, sunglasses and a hair barrette were scattered on the ground. Even more disturbing, the man's extendable police baton and the dog leash the young woman had been carrying were nearby.

Bill Clawson, another hiker out with family members, walked up as Blankenship studied the scene. He also had noticed the odd man lurking near the trail, as if waiting for Clawson's family to pass. They couldn't find the man, the young woman or anything else in the area, so Clawson gathered the scattered items and took them to a nearby store, in case anyone came looking for them. Blankenship searched for a while more, until dusk fell, and then left the park.

Meanwhile, the Union County Sheriff's Office and other responders were searching for Meredith, assuming that she was delayed or hurt on the trail. Late the following day, they called in the Georgia Bureau of Investigation.

Watching the news that evening, Clawson learned about Meredith's disappearance. He called the sheriff's office, then he drove in the middle of the night to the search command post on the mountain to let them know what he and Blankenship had seen on New Year's Day.

THE DAY GARY HILTON picked Meredith Emerson as his target was the beginning of the end of his predatory career. Hilton had been illegally camping in the state park for several days. He tended to live in the woods in a van littered with trash. He needed gas and food and was almost completely out of money, so he started looking for funds where he usually did: from someone he could rob. He targeted lone women because they were easier to intimidate or subdue. For him, women with dogs were easy to approach in isolated areas. Once he started complimenting her dog, the woman would tend to let down her guard and allow him to get closer than she might under other circumstances. And Hilton liked dogs, so they didn't tend to act aggressive or send up an alarm when he approached.

He would strike up a conversation, ask if the woman had friends with her. If she did, he backed off. With Meredith, he hiked a while with her on the trail, but she was too strong a hiker, so he dropped back. But as Bill Clawson had unwittingly observed, he was waiting when she came back down the trail, with a knife and an extendable police baton.

On January 3, authorities announced they were looking for the man seen hiking in the area with a dog. From the description, John Tabor knew who they were looking for. He called from near Atlanta to give them the name of his former employee: sixty-one-year-old Gary Hilton.

Other people in the area recognized the man from his description and knew that he drove a van like the one described in news bulletins. Those who had met Hilton described him as memorable. His face was lean and his gaze intense. He was often agitated, unable to keep still. His conversation rambled, with odd mixtures of conspiracies and rantings and observations whose connections were obvious only to him. In photos, he had a characteristic defiant stare.

He often wore a distinctive bright-yellow hiking jacket; he later said he liked to wear only the best, most expensive gear, obviously proud that it set him apart, although it also made a memorable contrast to his unkempt appearance.

In Florida, a hunter had seen a man fitting Hilton's description in the woods near where Cheryl Dunlap's body was found. Rangers had also spotted him in the area. Evidence was beginning to gather, leading to one man.

Four days after Meredith left to go hiking, anonymous tipsters called police from a convenience store in DeKalb County, Georgia: "The guy you are looking for is cleaning out his van." When police arrived, Hilton was throwing items into a trash dumpster behind the store, including Meredith's identification, her clothes and a bloodstained portion cut from a seatbelt in his van. They got there before he could wash or bleach the interior. Blood evidence from inside the van matched Meredith's DNA profile. They wouldn't know until later that he'd kept her alive while attempting to get money from her ATM account. He'd killed her the day he was arrested, January 4, four days after he kidnapped her.

Once police had him in custody, they had more trouble keeping him on topic than getting him to talk. He talked a lot, in rambling discourses about things that displeased him. The detective noticed that his hand was swollen about twice its normal size and offered medical attention. According to author Lee Butcher, Hilton told the doctor in the Atlanta Detention infirmary, "It's from punching that missing hiker. Fist against cranium. Don't worry, it hurt me a lot more than it hurt her." He told investigators, "She wouldn't stop. She wouldn't stop fighting. And yelling at the same time. So I needed to control her and silence her."

Hilton hadn't been able to get the correct ATM pin number from Meredith, so he held her hostage in his filthy van, later saying he thought she might have enjoyed the adventure—just one of many comments that raised the hackles of even seasoned investigators.

Hilton was initially surly and combative, but he was always calculating how to play the situation to his own benefit. When told he was being moved to North Georgia, he said he was relieved he'd be in a mostly white jail in a more rural area, but he also knew that meant his case would be handled by state, rather than federal, prosecutors. To him, this signaled that authorities were intent on getting the death penalty, so Hilton started bargaining. He agreed to take them to her body in exchange for removing the death penalty option.

Meredith's dog was found where Hilton abandoned her in Cummings, Georgia, about sixty miles from the hiking trail. That he'd left her dog alive and that she'd fought hard and made him lose his baton helped build the case against Hilton. The random crime scenes spread over three states would have been even more difficult to link without the physical evidence found at the scene on Blood Mountain and in the van.

The day after Hilton was indicted in Meredith's murder, Jack Bryant's remains were discovered in the Nantahala National Forest in North Carolina.

HILTON'S LIFE AND WORK history after he left the military were fraught with arrests and convictions for theft and drug possession, with three short-lived marriages, two lasting less than a year each. Something changed for him in 1997, when John Tabor hired him to work at Insulated Wall Systems. Hilton sold siding for the company, a largely self-directed job that seemed to suit his temperament. Tabor even gave him a place to live at the worksite. Starting at age fifty, Hilton's life settled into a somewhat regular routine.

Ten years later, that ended. Tabor filed a criminal complaint alleging that Hilton had tried to extort $10,000 from him and threatened to kill him if he didn't pay. For some reason, Hilton decided to wreck his decade of predictable housing and employment. After that, Hilton lived as a drifter and seemed to survive by stealing.

Before he found murder to be a more satisfying way to get money for his basic needs, before he started working for John Tabor selling siding, Hilton had another unusual job: a one-shot career as a movie consultant.

Samuel Rael, a Georgia lawyer, once represented Hilton in a legal matter. When Rael started working on a movie about a serial killer, Hilton proposed a plot about beautiful women hunted by a killer in the woods. IMDb, the online database for film and television, doesn't list Gary Hilton in the movie credits, but Rael said Hilton helped with the plot development and even found one of the movie's key shooting locations: a cabin in the mountains outside Cleveland, Georgia. When news broke about Hilton's arrest, even though Rael had represented him in court and knew he was a criminal, Rael couldn't see him as capable of violence.

The 1995 movie earned an unremarkable IMDb rating and never received much notice. But Hilton revisited the Dawson Forest area again when he dumped Meredith Emerson's body about thirty miles from the location of the movie cabin.

As THE INVESTIGATION UNFOLDED, investigators wondered if the apparent peacefulness of his life while working for Tabor was a sham. Evidence suggested that Hilton may have stalked and killed his first victim in 2005, a few years before he lost his job with Tabor. That missing hiker in North Carolina was added to a growing list of Hilton's possible victims. In December 2005, Rossana Miliani disappeared while staying at a hotel on Painttown Road in Cherokee, North Carolina. According to the online missing-person registry the Charley Project, Rossana had bipolar disorder and mild schizophrenia. But the vacationing twenty-nine-year-old from Miami had regularly called her father and kept him updated on her trip.

In her last call, her dad said, she planned to hike a portion of the Appalachian Trail and had even bought some gear for the adventure. The last known sighting of Rossana was on December 7, when she rented a storage space in Bryson City to hold items she'd brought with her from Florida while she hiked. Her suitcase, laptop, camera, cellphone and other belongings have never been found. Her bank account was never again accessed.

Two years later, when a store clerk belatedly learned about Rossana's disappearance, she contacted police. She recognized Rossana's photo.

N-412 CHEROKEE. N. C. BY MOONLIGHT.

NOBLE MOUNTAIN IN BACKGROUND

Vintage postcard of the town of Cherokee and its mountain backdrop. *Courtesy of Durwood Barbour Collection of North Carolina Postcards, UNC, and Asheville Post Card Company.*

Rossana had come into her store with a man who looked to be in his sixties. The clerk remembered her after all that time because she had looked scared or nervous, and it seemed unusual that she was traveling with this man. The man talked to the clerk a bit, told her that he was a traveling preacher visiting campgrounds in the area. The two bought some men's clothes and left.

ON APRIL 17, 2008, another investigator— this one from the sheriff's office in Pickens County, South Carolina—came to the Georgia Corrections Center to interview Hilton. Like any diligent investigator, when he'd seen headlines about the "National Forest Serial Killer," he thought about his ten-year-old cold case, the missing hiker case with no leads. On April 12, 1998, Jason Knapp, a Clemson University student, disappeared while hiking alone on Easter Sunday at Upstate South Carolina's Table Rock Park. No remains had been found, and he stayed on the list of missing persons cases the Pickens County investigator wanted to solve.

The athletic twenty-year-old Michigan native had transferred to Clemson to major in mechanical engineering. Jason had recently been inducted into the Pershing Rifle Corps, a military honor society and elite drill unit. The week after the Easter holiday, other ROTC members noted that he'd missed several classes and drills. His roommates last saw him the evening before Easter Sunday. The following Friday, his concerned friends called his mother to check on him.

On April 21, more than a week after Knapp left to go hiking, his car was found in the lot at Table Rock State Park, locked and undisturbed. A paper park pass inside, purchased Easter Sunday afternoon, yielded Jason's fingerprints. A ranger said he'd seen the car parked there for more than a week, but hikers sometimes forgot to sign into the trailhead register, so he hadn't raised an alarm.

The park offers easy day hikes, but the Pinnacle and Table Rock Trails are both strenuous, and either trail requires several hours to complete. It was

Table Rock State Park, with Table Rock Mountain in the background. *Courtesy of Mike Burton (scmikeburton) via Creative Commons and marked with CC BY-ND 2.0.*

unlikely Jason started at three o'clock that afternoon planning to tackle one of those. But where did he go?

Nothing indicated that he'd planned to disappear. He'd withdrawn twenty dollars from an ATM and then stopped by Wendy's and a grocery store, but his bank account hadn't been touched after that. His belongings, including his ROTC rifle and ammunition, were in his room. He'd left his laundry ready to carry to the laundromat.

Thousands of search hours in the park failed to find any sign of what happened to him, but the case had not been forgotten. For Captain Dewey Smith, the Pickens County investigator, the killer who attacked hikers was certainly a person of interest.

When Smith showed Hilton a photo of Jason Knapp, Hilton made some derisive comments about yuppies and metrosexuals and rambled, in his usual fashion, before touching on something that might, or might not, have been truthful. He acknowledged that the disappearance seemed to fit the "modus operandi that I am assumed to have used in several crimes that I am suspected of." He said he wanted to reassure them that "if I knew anything that had happened to your son, I would not refuse to answer."

He continued to ramble, piling words upon words, and then said he was suspected in two North Carolina murders and one in Florida. "I am not going to tell you I did those, but I am telling you is, I'm not telling anybody I didn't do them, okay? I'm not saying I didn't do them, but what I'm saying is there's nothing outside those three murders, no nothing."

Was he telling the truth? What about Rossana Miliani, who planned to hike part of the Appalachian Trail and was seen in the company of a man who fit Hilton's description just when she disappeared? Hilton had nothing to say about other cases.

In 2008, Hilton pleaded guilty in a Georgia court to killing Meredith Emerson and received a life sentence; he would be eligible for parole in thirty years—when he would be ninety-one years old.

In 2011, a jury in Florida found him guilty of killing Cheryl Dunlap, and he received the death penalty. The appellate court upheld his sentence. As of 2021, he was on death row in Union Correctional Institution (formerly Raiford Prison and Florida State Prison).

Because the kidnapping and killing of the Bryants occurred on federal land, Hilton appeared in a North Carolina federal court. In 2013, he received four life sentences for those crimes with no possibility of parole.

More than a decade after Hilton's capture, those involved in the case continued to dwell on the near misses and what-might-have-beens of the case. In 2020, John Cagle, the supervising GBI agent who worked Meredith's disappearance, wrote a book about the case. Cagle wanted to describe the case from an investigator's perspective, rather than a journalist reporting it at arm's length. No one who worked it would ever forget, he said.

In an interview with the *Dawson News*, Cagle said that one distinctive feature of the investigation was how the community turned out to help. From the alert hikers on the trail the day Meredith was kidnapped to Hilton's former employer, the many tipsters who called in with sightings and information and all who physically searched for the missing woman, Cagle was impressed with the caring response. In particular, he said, those who frequent the Appalachian Trail form a unique community, and the word went out quickly on their network. "That was kind of refreshing," Cagle said. "When you're in the criminal justice business, you don't see a lot of that."

One woman later completed a speed hike of the Appalachian Trail to honor Meredith and the Bryants, in an attempt to remove some of the taint

Hilton had left for those who loved the Trail. Hikes and 5K-race fundraisers were held, and a trail was named after Meredith.

The investigators as well as Meredith's family and friends also second-guess whether she could have been saved, had clues been followed faster, had they known who and what they were looking for. In Cagle's book, he included some of what Hilton said, in his own words, during his numerous and lengthy interviews. Hilton's rambling, self-absorbed statements hint that no one could have truly known what they were dealing with, not until he was captured and started talking. Cagle said it was "pretty scary for people, to give a look at how evil he is by some of his own quotes."

One thing those close to the case know is that Meredith Emerson saved lives. She fought Hilton, causing him to scatter items beside the Blood Mountain Trail. She convinced him that she was giving him the correct ATM pin numbers, encouraging him to try again, hoping that a trail of failed transactions would alert police or provide a photo of him on an ATM camera.

GBI director Vernon Keenan told the *Atlanta Journal-Constitution,* "She nearly got the best of him. She's very much a hero."

ERIC RUDOLPH

The wilderness of Western North Carolina and the home-grown terrorist who attracted international headlines are inseparably linked.

Eric Rudolph spent most of his growing up years around Marble, North Carolina, a small town in the westernmost section of the state between Andrews and Murphy. His upbringing has been closely scrutinized by those looking for clues to what formed him, but whatever the influences, Eric grew up with a distrust of the government that eventually spilled over into violence. A distrust of government isn't an uncommon trait among those born in these mountains, a trait that was generations in the making. Eric Rudolph, for his own reasons, turned that anger and distrust into action.

The story began with what promoters hoped would be an event of great civic boosterism. Against the odds, Atlanta beat out Athens, Greece—home of the ancient Greek games and of the first modern Olympic Games—to host the centennial celebration of the Olympics in 1996. For the celebration, corporate sponsors made record-setting investments in the venues. Muhammad Ali lit the torch at the opening ceremonies. Amid much talk

Atlanta's Centennial Olympic Park. *Courtesy of Kirt Morris on Unsplash.com.*

about the high security planned for the event, Eric Rudolph knew that this was the place to make a big statement.

On July 26, 1996, the country-fair section inside the security perimeter was crowded with people getting food at the booths, people-watching or resting between events. A man dressed in a blue short-sleeved shirt and jeans carried a large military-style Alice backpack through the security checkpoint. He found the spot he wanted: a bench tucked away near the music stage sound tower. He put his bag on the ground, unzipped it and set the Westclox alarm clock inside to go off in fifty-five minutes. Then he pushed the pack under the bench, got up and left.

The pack contained Tupperware containers holding three pipe bombs loaded with gunpowder and steel nails, an igniter for a model rocket engine, an Eveready six-volt battery and the alarm clock. The bomb was designed to cause maximum damage, with a steel plate inserted against the rear of the pack to focus the force of the blast and the shrapnel out into the crowd. This was only the first of five bombs he planned to leave around Olympic venues.

Whatever Eric Rudolph's motives, he could predict that his bombs would kill and maim people. He couldn't predict the damage to security guard Richard Jewell, who was first called a hero and then became a target, thanks to media hungry for a story about a shadowy man no one could find fast enough to fill the 24/7 news cycle. The feeding frenzy was fierce, and the would-be hero was the only fresh meat available.

As Richard Jewell walked his patrol route through Centennial Park that night, noise from a rowdy bunch of guys attracted his attention to the area near the bench and then to the lone backpack. He asked if it belonged to any of those nearby. He got on the radio and called a GBI agent working security to help him.

Before the bomb team could arrive, Jewell began warning people in the multi-story sound tower about the suspicious package. With all the security warnings in and around the park to be on the alert for abandoned packages, Jewell was paying attention and doing his job.

Security cleared a perimeter around the bench so the bomb team could work. A member of the team crawled under the bench to get a look inside the bag. "It's big," he said as he carefully slid back out. About the same time they found the bomb, 911 logged a call at 12:57 a.m. from a payphone located blocks from the park: "There is a bomb in Centennial Park. You have thirty minutes."

As it turned out, they didn't have quite that much time before the backpack exploded. The one death caused directly by the bomb was forty-four-year-old Alice Hawthorne, who had brought her stepdaughter from Albany, Georgia, to enjoy the landmark event. More than one hundred others were injured and taken to hospitals. Melih Uzunyol, a Turkish cameraman covering the games, died of a heart attack as he ran to film the scene.

Jewell's attention and quick action saved lives. The accolades lasted until the *Atlanta Journal-Constitution* reported that he was the focus of the FBI's investigation. National and international media picked up the story, digging into the similarities he shared with the FBI profile of the bomber and his reputation as an overzealous wanna-be cop.

The FBI eventually cleared him, but the damaging news reports cost Jewell a lot—harassment, public humiliation, jobs and more. Attorney Lin Wood began to advise Jewell and sued several media companies for libel, including CNN, NBC and the Atlanta newspaper where it had all started. In 2019, Clint Eastwood's film *Richard Jewell* was released, detailing the personal cost to him and his mother. Kent Alexander, the *Wall Street Journal* writer who co-wrote the book *The Suspect*, called Jewell perhaps the first victim of the 24/7 news cycle. Jewell's response that night was eventually given official recognition when he was honored at Georgia's capitol, ten years after the Olympic bombing.

When the Jewell lead didn't pan out, authorities knew they still had a bomber on the loose. No terrorist or radical group took credit for the bombing. The FBI had no intelligence from inside any subversive group.

No one could describe the man with the backpack. The lab was still studying the bomb components looking for clues.

In January 1997, six months after the Olympic bombing, another bomb went off outside an abortion clinic in Sandy Springs, in north-central Atlanta. This time, a second bomb detonated just as police and fire were responding to the scene. Fortunately, no one was injured.

In February, a third bomb exploded in the parking lot at the Otherside Lounge, a bar on Piedmont Road in Atlanta that catered to a lesbian clientele. Five people were injured in the explosion. Police, on alert for a second backpack device, found it in the parking lot and used a robot to detonate it.

Despite the destructive force of a bomb, individual bomb components survive and provide valuable forensic evidence about the source of those components and who put them together. Now the FBI had the components from three different bomb sites to study, and it gained one key piece of information: they were all made by the same person.

On January 29, 1998, outside an abortion clinic in Birmingham, Alabama, nurse Emily Lyons and off-duty police officer Sandy Sanderson were coming to work when they spotted a FedEx package stuck in the shrubs near the front door. When Sandy bent over the box, the bomb exploded. He was killed instantly. Emily Lyons was left with serious and permanent disfiguring wounds to her face and body.

Sometimes a criminal's simplest mistake can be his most costly. In Alabama, the bomber detonated the package by remote control, which meant he was nearby, watching Sandy and Emily arrive at work. When the bomb exploded, most people in the vicinity headed toward the noise to see what had happened. A college student noticed one man walking calmly in the opposite direction. That seemed an odd reaction, so he got in his car to get a look at the man and then ran into a McDonald's to call 911.

Another customer overheard his phone call, ran out to his car, followed the man and got the license tag number on his truck. The student's awareness of the man's odd behavior and the willingness of citizens to get involved proved the turning point.

Bombs are meant to send a message. They are frightening in their randomness and lethal in their power. The ability to manufacture a bomb that can be safely transported and detonated at the optimal time takes knowledge and practice. For a bomber, practice makes perfect. And whoever this bomber was, he was getting plenty of practice.

But what message was he trying to send? Was he anti-abortion? Then why attack at the Olympic Games? Was he anti-American? Why bomb a gay bar? Maybe the clearest clue came with the second and third bombings in Atlanta. At the Sandy Springs abortion clinic and again at the Otherside Lounge, the initial bombs were followed by second, much stronger blasts, timed to target police and other authorities responding to the scene.

The license tag number from the Alabama incident gave authorities a name: Eric Robert Rudolph. The FBI alerted regional law enforcement in Western North Carolina and started searching in Asheville, where the car was registered. Sheriff Jack Thompson in Cherokee County called to tell the FBI he'd learned that Eric Rudolph was renting a trailer in his area. In a later interview with Dr. Cynthia Lewis, a Davidson College English professor who researched the case, the sheriff said he'd called around to the area post offices and the power company to see if they were providing service to an Eric Rudolph or Randolph, one of Eric's aliases. Old-fashioned detective work gave him the rental address.

The FBI asked Sheriff Thompson to hold off on approaching the cabin. They needed to carefully prepare. Some said the FBI wanted to grab the glory for capturing Rudolph. Sheriff Thompson told Dr. Lewis he was later glad he and his deputies hadn't rushed to the trailer. Rudolph was dangerous and desperate.

Unfortunately, the news of the lead somehow leaked to CNN. When the law officers approached the trailer, they found the door open and the TV tuned to the broadcast. The food on the kitchen table and the $1,600 in cash on the counter suggested that they'd missed him by just minutes and that he'd left in a hurry.

Along with law enforcement, the news media descended on the little town of Andrews with more than sixty satellite trucks and microphones seeking anyone who could give them a sound bite for the evening news.

In May 1998, the FBI put Rudolph on its Most Wanted list, and the federal government posted a $1 million reward for information leading to his capture.

THOSE UNFAMILIAR WITH NORTH Carolina's Southern Appalachian Mountains have trouble imagining a place where a man could elude determined searchers for years. The tree canopy is too thick for search planes, the terrain too steep to hike easily and the vegetation often thick and impenetrable. Although the mountains attract hunters and hikers, vacationers escaping the heat and retirees flocking to golf communities, much of mountainous Western North Carolina is wild. The trails and peaks may lie close to roads and towns, but proximity doesn't make the wildest parts easy to access. Unless trails are maintained, as in the state and national parklands, the slopes and valleys are often taken over by *Rhododendron maximum*. The lush shrub grows in large, dense, impenetrable masses that produce clusters of white to pink flowers in the heat of summer. Those who grow up in the area know them as laurels rather than rhododendron, and they know to avoid crawling into the dense jungle of shrubs, known as "laurel hells," because summer heat is oppressive inside the branches and because it is almost impossible to fight your way back out.

Bears and snakes are the primary wildlife threats, although those threats are minimal. The more likely risks are hypothermia in winter, dehydration in summer, disorientation, injury from a fall and dramatic changes in the weather, bringing high winds, felled trees, flash floods and steep drops in temperature. As with any wilderness area, whether high alpine regions in the Rockies or a desert, the Southern Appalachians present their own challenges and risks, along with their beauty.

Eric Rudolph knew those mountains well, and he knew how to survive. In the years he stayed on the run, speculation was rampant. Were people back

SCENE ON THE MURPHY LINE, IN THE LAND OF THE SKY.

A 1913 postcard of Murphy. *Courtesy of Durwood Barbour Collection of North Carolina Postcards, UNC, and Brown Book Company, Asheville.*

in the mountains helping him? Had he established bolt holes and stored supplies if he needed to hide? Was he dead? Had he left the country?

The jokes were rampant too. T-shirts and bumper stickers showed a reindeer approaching a federal agent, "I hear you're looking for Rudolph." Others named Rudolph the "National Hide and Seek Champion."

During a sabbatical from teaching and a few years after the hunt began, Dr. Lewis spent months conducting her interviews. She talked to people, built relationships and gathered their stories for her detailed article about how the search affected and was perceived by the residents.

Lewis interviewed Kenny Cope, who'd known Eric since they were teens and who, when the search was ongoing, was a deputy sheriff in Macon County. Cope said, "CNN's Eric's best friend. If it hadn't been for the media, Eric Rudolph would have been caught in the first two days. The media's the worst thing that ever happened to this case. The worst thing."

In the months after federal agents took up residence in the county, vowing to stay until Rudolph was captured, two men shot at the Andrews command post. An agent was injured slightly. The men were captured and convicted. A local law officer told Lewis, "I think Jack Daniels, Barley Corn and 'Thunderchief' were also involved. Apparently this was some kind of rampage aimed at the task force that had nothing to do with Eric Rudolph. Sobriety had nothing to do with it either."

While the mountain culture and his family helped nurture and make Eric Rudolph, the mountains also hid him. For five years, he scavenged food from vacation and hunting cabins little used by their owners and filled his backpack with grain from a local granary to carry away and store in fifty-five-gallon drums buried in the ground. He used multiple storage and campsites and knew the mountains well enough to move around at night.

He later told FBI interrogators that the first year was the worst. In his confession, he said that year "was a starving time." But then he developed a routine, including knowing the best nights to check the restaurants in town for fresh vegetables in crates on their loading docks and edible discards in their dumpsters. He also had caches of dynamite buried in locations scattered in the mountains. From hilltop lookouts, he kept an eye on those hunting for him and continued to concoct plans for more attacks—first on the large command center of FBI agents searching for him and on another abortion clinic—but he never carried out those attacks.

In a fitting conclusion for a story about a fugitive eluding a massive, multimillion-dollar search, the end came quietly, with one young officer taking pains to do his job. When law enforcement and searchers first

One of the caches of nitroglycerine dynamite hidden in the mountains by Eric Rudolph. *Released by the Federal Bureau of Investigation.*

descended on Andrews in 1998, Jeff Postell was a high school student working at McDonald's and wanting to someday be a police officer.

Five years later, Postell was a ten-month rookie police officer for the town of Murphy, about fifteen miles from Andrews and as far west as you can go in North Carolina and still live in a town. At about 3:30 a.m. on May 31, 2003, while driving patrol on the night shift, he pulled up behind a grocery store. Not every officer does that, but Postell liked to go by the book.

He saw someone rummaging in a dumpster. In the dim light, he glimpsed something long in the man's hand as he dodged for cover behind a stack of milk crates on the loading dock. Postell pulled his gun and ordered him to the ground. The man carried a large flashlight, not a gun. He said he was homeless, just looking for food. He gave a fake name and had no ID or address. Something just didn't feel right to Postell, so he took him to the station and put him in a cell.

Another officer thought that he looked like Eric Rudolph. Postell pulled up the FBI's Most Wanted site. Other officers gathered around. They printed a copy of the wanted poster and took it back to where the handcuffed man was sitting. They held the photo up and studied the man's face. One officer asked him who he was.

The prisoner replied, "What does the paper say?"

Postell later said, "And with a little snicker he looked up and says, 'I'm Eric Robert Rudolph, and you've got me.'"

Postell told Jeremy Markovich in a 2019 *Our State* magazine interview that, at the time, he had no idea he would become part of the story. He got fan mail. *People* magazine named him one of 2003's hottest bachelors. Motorists wanted him write them tickets so they would have his autograph.

The FBI's wanted poster for Eric Rudolph. *Released by the Federal Bureau of Investigation.*

Markovich interviewed Postell after he'd taken a job as an officer at Boston College and settled down in Boston—with his office next to campus police chief Bill Evans, who coincidentally led the search for the Boston Marathon bombers, making the two officers a unique team of terrorist-bomber catchers.

On April 13, 2005, to avoid the death penalty, Rudolph entered his guilty plea for all four bombings and told officials where he'd hidden 250 pounds of dynamite in the mountains. He was sentenced to four life sentences; the federal system does not provide for parole. He was sent to the "Alcatraz of the Rockies," the federal Administrative Maximum Facility (ADX) in Florence, Colorado, which also houses domestic terrorists Oklahoma City bomber Terry Nichols and Unabomber Ted Kaczynski, international terrorist Boston bomber Dzhokhar Tsarnaev and Robert Hanssen, the FBI agent who spied for the Soviets.

Travis Dusenbury, a Lexington, North Carolina native who also served time at Supermax, as it's known, described the desolation of that prison: "You can't see nothing, not a highway out in the distance, not the sky. You're just shut off from the world. You feel it. It sinks in, this dread feeling. It's just the harshest place you've ever seen. Nothing living, not so much as a blade of grass anywhere."

Most Supermax prisoners are confined to single cells made entirely of concrete, including the bed, for twenty-three hours a day. Most are allowed to walk outside in a cage for an hour or two a day, alone.

Dusenbury, who is African American, got to know Rudolph inside Supermax and said, "I appreciated him because he could have easily gotten cozy with the Aryan Brotherhood, but he didn't, he talked to me. He was a gentleman, and that's one thing we can all get with at the ADX."

Dusenbury said that one form of communication for prisoners was the toilet telephone—they could talk to an adjoining cell through the toilet plumbing after blowing through a toilet paper roll to clear out the water. Or they talked or did "finger handshakes" through the chain link fences in the exercise cages.

For a man like Eric Rudolph who loved the thick, green woods of the Appalachian Mountains, Supermax would indeed be a prison.

THE PISGAH INN MURDER

The original Pisgah Inn opened in 1918, not far from where wealthy industrialist George Vanderbilt and owner of the Biltmore Estate maintained Buck Springs Lodge, a rustic log hunting lodge. The current inn, built in 1964, commands stunning views from a high ridge at the Blue Ridge Parkway's Milepost 408.6, on a section that opened in the 1960s. The inn boasts lodging at five thousand feet, the highest elevation for lodging along the parkway, and many visitors hike to the peak of neighboring Mount Pisgah.

For more than one hundred years, tourists have come to this spot to escape the summer heat and enjoy the views from the porches or from the window-lined restaurant.

A 1907 postcard of George Vanderbilt's hunting lodge near Mount Pisgah. *Courtesy of Durwood Barbour Collection of North Carolina Postcards, UNC, and Souvenir Post Card Company, New York.*

Completed in 1965, Pisgah Inn's balconies overlook the vista below. *Courtesy of Library of Congress, Prints and Photographs Division.*

In the spring of 2018, twenty-nine-year-old Sara Ellis left her family in Florida to take a seasonal chef's job at the Inn, which operated from April to October. Sara loved to cook for family and friends, and her chocolate cake was a favorite. She hoped one day to run her own restaurant, and the job at Pisgah would be a great first step on that road.

Sara had grown up around Melbourne, but the family lived for a time in Asheville. Her mother died when Sara was in her early twenties, and a return to the North Carolina mountains probably felt like a return to happier times when the family was together. She already had an associate degree and had worked in university food service and restaurant jobs. Next, she wanted a degree in restaurant management, and working at Pisgah would give her additional hands-on experience.

Since her teens, Sara had dealt with a severe hearing impairment, but friends knew her as a person of deep faith who looked for the positive and saw opportunities within the challenges. She communicated regularly with her sisters and friends after she got to Pisgah, telling them how beautiful it was, that she was enjoying living in the staff dorm and was making friends. Pisgah was about forty minutes from either Waynesville or Asheville, so the forty or so seasonal staff lived on site. While nightlife and shopping required a long drive, the area offered hiking trails and vistas galore.

On Tuesday, July 24, 2018, Sara got off work about four o'clock in the afternoon. A few hours later, twenty-year-old Derek Shawn Pendergraft, who worked at the inn as a housekeeper, went to the manager's office to report Sara missing. He said the two of them left after work to hike one of the trails. When it started raining, Sara decided to turn back, but he kept walking. Later, when he was returning to the dorm, he found her umbrella and hat on the trail but couldn't find any sign of her.

Rangers and investigators arrived to search the area as the summer night darkened. At about 10:30 p.m., they found her body along a trail near the staff lodging. She had been beaten and strangled and was partially undressed.

Those living at beautiful but isolated Mount Pisgah didn't have long to speculate or fret about what happened. The next evening, Pendergraft returned to the inn's manager and confessed to killing Sara. He told FBI investigators that he had blacked out for a time on the trail. When he came to his senses, he saw Sara, dead.

Her family and friends were stunned. She'd told them how beautiful the place was. She even texted her sister just days before her death: "This is a safe place." None of them remembered her mentioning Pendergraft among those friends she was getting to know, and no one at the inn knew of any plans they had to go hiking after work.

Initially, Pendergraft was charged with second-degree murder, upgraded to first degree when the autopsy revealed the violence of the attack. That Sara was functionally deaf made imagining her last moments even worse for her sisters, family and friends.

One year later, in August 2019, Pendergraft pleaded guilty to first-degree murder and two counts of aggravated sexual abuse. The case was heard in federal court because the offense happened on federal land.

As Tiffany Coleman, Sara's elder sister, told the court what a kind person Sara was and how proud she'd been when Sara ventured out to follow her dream with the job at Pisgah Inn, Pendergraft sat with his lawyers, his head in his hands. His court-appointed federal public defender referred to his juvenile file, which the judge saw but which was sealed to the public and the press, and pointed out "how he got here." While Pendergraft's criminal record was clean, apparently his file detailed other issues that affected his ability to function normally.

The judge said, "The defendant has a truly sad background and has had experiences in life that have given him no real opportunity to develop as a normal child." He called it "among the saddest" cases he's seen, for the families on both sides. He sentenced Pendergraft to three life sentences without parole but also said he hoped treatment for his mental health, substance abuse and sex offender issues would be a benefit to him. He would serve his time in federal custody.

The case could have happened anywhere. That it happened where many come for renewal and recreation overlooking beautiful vistas made headlines.

SIDE TRIPS, CRIME BITS AND ODDITIES

THE 120-YEAR-OLD SHOOTING

Over time, buildings take on different uses, and even the most astonishing stories fade from memory. Opened in 1979, a popular Cashiers restaurant boasts an enormous covered dining porch to take advantage of cool summer breezes. Customers lining up for lunch may miss the little sign announcing that the restaurant is attached to what was, one hundred years ago, Evan Pell's general store.

The Pells were stalwarts in the Cashiers community. Evan Pell and his wife, Elizabeth Coats Bryson Allison Pell, lived across the street from the store in a building that now serves as an office. From the vantage of the slight rise where their home sat, she could keep tabs on the comings and goings at the store. What she saw and heard on one muggy, overcast August day in 1901 concerned her: yelling, arguing, building tensions and too much drinking.

She walked across Highway 107 to the store and told father and son Columbus and Javan Long and the rest of them to clear out—time to go home. She knew every man in the group, and her husband as well, all carried guns, and the heat and the drinking and the tempers were about to boil over.

That was exactly what happened late that afternoon. The Longs returned to the store. Columbus Long fired a ball from a steel slingshot and hit Evan Pell in the head, then Javan shot Evan twice with his pistols. After Evan

Left: Plaque commemorating Evan Pell's store in Cashiers. *Photo by J.D. Dickinson.*

Below: House where Pell's family lived, across Highway 107 from their store. *Photo by Cathy Pickens.*

stumbled and fell in the road, Columbus hit him in the head again with another slingshot ball.

Doctors who later examined Evan's body said the head wounds from the slingshot—used as a hunting weapon, not a toy—would have killed him even if he hadn't also taken two slugs. Javan headed for distant parts—reportedly dressed as a woman—but he was eventually tried and served five years in prison.

Evan Pell's former store has been home to the Cornucopia Restaurant since 1979. *Photo by Cathy Pickens.*

The Cashiers Historical Society preserved Evan Pell's story, along with the many others from Cashiers's colorful and sometimes tragic history. Photos from 1914 show that the former store has changed little in the last century. Few who come to Cornucopia for a hamburger or piece of buttermilk pie likely imagine a drunken shooting raging just outside the front door on Highway 107.

MOVIE WRECKS

The 1993 film *The Fugitive* was based on a real-life true crime case, and one of the movie's most iconic scenes was filmed outside Dillsboro, along the rail line operated by the Great Smoky Mountains Railroad.

In the real case, Dr. Sam Sheppard, an Ohio surgeon, was accused in 1954 of killing his wife. He claimed that a mysterious, bushy-haired man surprised the couple in their home, knocked him unconscious and bludgeoned her to

Remaining set where prison bus carrying actor Harrison Ford collided with a train in *The Fugitive*, filmed on Great Smoky Mountain Railroad. *Photo by Cathy Pickens.*

death. The prosecutor and police didn't buy his story, and a jury convicted him in what was later called "a trial by newspaper." Soon-to-be-famous defense attorney F. Lee Bailey got involved in Sheppard's appeal, arguing that the intense media coverage had influenced the outcome. The U.S. Supreme Court agreed and ordered a new trial, citing the trial's carnival atmosphere. The decision set a precedent for future high-profile trials and put judges on alert that what goes on outside the courtroom can influence what happens inside.

At the second trial, Bailey called the prosecutor's case "ten pounds of hogwash in a five-pound bag." The jury acquitted Dr. Sheppard.

None of that happened in Western North Carolina. But when filmmakers decided to make a movie based on the popular 1960s TV show *The Fugitive*, the Great Smoky Mountains Railroad became the scene of a train/bus collision and the escape of Harrison Ford (as Dr. Sheppard), on the run to find the real killer.

In the early 1990s, computer generated effects weren't fully developed, so the filmmakers had to wreck a real train—or a hollow model of a real train—on real train tracks.

To visit the wreck scene, book a trip on the Tuckasegee River excursion between Bryson City and Dillsboro, which follows along one of the most beautiful mountain rivers in the country. (See https://www.gsmr.com/tuckasegee for dates and times.) The train doesn't stop at the wreck site, but the train and bus wreckage are still where the moviemakers left them.

The region played host to another famous movie crash scene in 1957—this one at the same site as a real-life tragedy. Buncombe and Transylvania Counties served as stand-ins for Tennessee in the Robert Mitchum movie *Thunder Road*. Mitchum plays a moonshine runner hunted by federal agents. In one chase scene, a car runs off the top of Toxaway Falls and smashes to pieces on the rocks below.

To keep everyone safe during the filming, that stunt wasn't done with a driver. The car was shoved off the top of the falls, with some manual dismantling after it came to rest at the bottom. In a film known for its speeding cars and explosions, the car off the falls is a classic scene.

The Toxaway Falls area also saw dramatic events even without movie cameras present. Before the first bridge was built over Toxaway Falls, the unpaved road forded the river above the falls. In 1916, a record-breaking flood hit Western North Carolina, the result of the confluence of two tropical storms, one moving from the Gulf Coast and one from the Atlantic. The floodwaters hit unexpectedly and washed out the three bridges crossing the French Broad in Asheville, causing record flooding as far away as Charlotte. The earthen dam that contained Lake Toxaway collapsed, emptying the lake in half an hour. Fortunately, the land downstream in South Carolina could handle the volume of water without much damage. Although some had to make desperate escapes from the floodwaters, a horse was the only reported casualty.

According to local historian T.W. Reynolds, Toxaway Falls did claim two lives in a mysterious accident sometime in the 1950s. A car sat alone near the

Catastrophic 1916
Asheville flooding.
*Courtesy of Durwood
Barbour Collection of North
Carolina Postcards, UNC.*

top of the falls long enough that locals became concerned. Someone looked over the rock shelf to search for the owners and saw two bodies below. A dentist and his wife, visiting the area on a day trip, had started to climb down to the pools below the falls. Apparently the wife slipped and grabbed her husband. Both were killed.

Those driving over the falls today would scarcely know that the beautiful falls exist. The smooth, broad bridge is much safer but far different from the passage one hundred years ago—or the one captured on film.

Brown Mountain Lights

Mysterious lights appearing on Brown Mountain have been explained in Cherokee legends, studied by paranormal investigators, academic scientists, the U.S. Weather Service and the U.S. Geological Survey and dissected in TV documentaries and magazine articles, including a cover story in the December 1968 issue of *Argosy*.

The lights appear as red balls (or green or blue or yellow), lasting for only a few seconds, moving among the trees or floating above the mountain. Are they car lights (even though they were first spotted long before car lights existed)? Swamp gas from decaying plant material? Some sort of emission from rock fissures near Linville Caverns or deep earth movement exciting the quartz crystals in the bedrock? Ghosts? Passing aliens in UFOs? A psychic vortex or liminal space for movement between astral planes? In researcher and tour operator Joshua Warren's booklet *Brown Mountain Lights*, he explores much of the research and speculation on what causes the lights.

Visit the overlook, located north of Morganton and east of Spruce Pine, and see what you can see. From the Brown Mountain Overlook between

Mysterious lights have been seen on Brown Mountain, which sits in the center of the photo. At the far left is the taller Chestnut Mountain. *Photo by Cathy Pickens.*

mile markers 20 and 21 on N.C. Highway 181, enjoy a nice view of Chestnut Mountain, the largest mountain visible. Brown Mountain sits to its right. The best time is just at dusk or early dark, ideally during peak leaf season in the fall. But be aware that the lights don't appear for everyone.

Judaculla Rock

Although Judaculla Rock—one of the largest petroglyphs in the United States—offers no crime, it offers plenty of mystery. The soapstone rock is sixteen by eleven feet in size and covered with carvings. Who created them and when, how exactly they were made and what they symbolize seem destined to remain unknown.

The Cherokees used soapstone from this area for pipes, bowls and other utensils, but these carvings existed long before the Cherokees inhabited these mountains and valleys. Some researchers believe that the stone may be part of a larger grouping that was buried by soil accretion over time. The rock's name comes from a Cherokee legend about Tsul'kalu', the Great Slant-Eyed Giant, a hunter of mythical size and ability who lived on Richland Balsam Mountain, the largest mountain in the Balsam

152

Judaculla Rock, with ancient petroglyphs carved in the soapstone, sits off Highway 107 outside Cullowhee. *Courtesy of QueenofFrogs via Creative Commons and marked with CC BY-SA 4.0.*

chain. No road or trail runs between the mountain and the rock, but what's distance over mountainous terrain to a giant? One legend says he didn't need to walk. He simply jumped from his mountain and landed on the rock, marking it forever.

Jackson County owns the land where the rock sits. The site is a little more than ten miles outside Sylva, off the road from Cashiers.

Mountain Witches and Graveyard Rabbits

Witches? In the mountains? The Southern Appalachians have a long tradition of "granny witches" who served their communities as healers skilled with herbs and home cures. But the mountains also have their ghostly traditions: demon dogs that lurk along trails when the moon is dark or the terrifying graveyard rabbits.

A tale of a graveyard rabbit was preserved by none other than Uncle Remus, who warned that graveyard rabbits were witches in disguise and couldn't be killed with a regular shotgun. Although Uncle Remus stories came from central Georgia, graveyard rabbits were also known in the mountains of North Carolina. Common wisdom said that the rabbits were to be avoided, although some felt they were transformed good witches and could bring inspiration or aid to "conjured ones" affected by evil.

In 1900, *Atlanta Constitution* columnist Frank Lebby Stanton published "The Graveyard Rabbit," and the rabbit in his poem, "though sceptics scoff, Charmeth the witch and the wizard off!" Sadly for rabbits, these mystical powers are the likely source of the superstition about lucky rabbits' feet.

Sylva's Goat Gland Doctor

Most would label Dr. John Brinkley a fraud—after all, he wasn't even a doctor, although he convinced plenty of people that he was. Had he also convinced himself? Are you practicing a fraud if you genuinely believe that the medical treatments you perform are helping people? Was John Brinkley a true believer in his goat gland treatment?

Brinkley was born in Beta, North Carolina, a community outside Sylva, in 1885. His aunt raised him after his mother died. He went from working as a telegraph operator to enrolling in Chicago's Bennett Medical College. He left without finishing, but that didn't stop him from setting up practice in Greenville, South Carolina.

In 1913, in a second-story office near Coffee and Main, Brinkley and a partner offered invigorating treatments with his Magno-Electric Vitalizer at $25 a jolt—about $700 today. Brinkley and his partner left Greenville after a legal tussle—not for medical fraud but rather for bouncing bad checks.

He later moved to Arkansas and graduated from the Eclectic Medical University, a name of great prestige and promise, but in practice, it gave away degrees to those who would pay for the privilege of a piece of official-looking paper.

Not until his late thirties did Brinkley develop the procedure that brought fame and fortune for him and promised a rejuvenated sex life and the elusive fountain of youth for his patients. By 1918, he operated a clinic in Milford, Kansas. Did being in a farming community spark his imagination? Or his time as a physician at a meatpacking plant? Did a farmer actually suggest the procedure to him? Whatever his inspiration, he hit on a cure for what ailed his patients.

He convinced others—and perhaps himself—that he was riding the wave of glandular medicine. While the sales pitch sounded enticing, the technique itself was squirm-inducing. In a surgical theater, he took the sex glands of goats and inserted them into the abdomen of patients desperate

HE'S FIRST GOAT-GLAND BABY

Dr. John Brinkley and one of the goat-gland babies. *Photo from the Arizona Republican (Phoenix), February 20, 1920, courtesy of the Library of Congress.*

to cure their impotence. His miracle "sex secret" began drawing patients from hundreds of miles for his $750 procedures (about $9,000 today).

While the American Medical Association labeled him and his miracle cures as frauds, his patients weren't listening. They lined up at his private hospital, the one with pens of Toggenberg goats in the back.

He soon stopped offering to cure women of infertility—a baby was too substantive a measure of success. And producing no baby was clearly a failure. Men, though, could be revitalized repeatedly and be none the wiser, apparently.

Brinkley believed in advertising to get the word out and eventually owned one of the first radio stations in Kansas with enough broadcast power to reach plenty of potential patients. Inevitably, though, the medical malpractice lawsuits began to stack up, and a watchdog from the American Medical Association began hounding his practice.

Brinkley decamped over the border to Mexico, ran a radio station powerful enough to broadcast to Canada, boosted the musical careers of hometown mountainfolk like the Carter family, inspired the Brinkleyism political movement in Kansas and finally returned to Jackson County to buy a summer home in the mountains. With the fortune accumulated from his various enterprises, he bought thousands of acres of mountain property around what had once been home. He also erected two roadside markers on the narrow verge between Highway 107 and the Tuckasegee River near East Laporte, to honor his mother and his aunt Sally, who was like a mother to him.

Facing lawsuits and tax evasion charges, he died bankrupt in 1942 and was buried in Memphis. The goat gland doctor made his mark wherever he went, but Western North Carolina was always his home. The doctor and his career continue to draw interest. Pope Brock's book, *Charlatan*, provides a well-researched and entertaining look at the span of Brinkley's career. In 2016, the memorably titled *Nuts!*, an animated "mostly true" documentary, debuted.

Golden Age Mystery in Highlands

In a region filled with mystery, surely someone wrote a Golden Age mystery novel set in Western North Carolina, with its glowering mountains and unique characters? Not about a real crime, but one of those stylish novels of the kind written by Agatha Christie, Dorothy L. Sayers, Anthony Berkeley and Josephine Tey, whose play-fair mysteries featured exotic settings, suspects galore and a puzzle for the reader to solve. What better place than the Appalachian Mountains?

Proprietor Stuart Ferguson at Shakespeare and Company Bookseller in Highlands asked that very question. He had a personal passion for Golden Age mysteries, whose popularity began between the world wars. And his own book sleuthing solved the mystery.

Dorothy Ogburn, one of the many seasonal residents who came to Highlands from Atlanta every summer, penned *Death on the Mountain* in 1931. The cozy cast of well-drawn mountain characters, visitors and a birdwatcher who spotted a buzzard near a corpse take the quintessential British country house mystery formula and translate it to the fictional small mountain town of Thunder Falls—Highlands in 1925, by any other name.

As with many Golden Age mysteries, the mystery is puzzling and fun to solve, a nice respite from real-life crime.

The Land of Oz

Take the popularity of immense theme parks like Disneyland and Disney World, shrink the land to a few acres and stir in a healthy dose of roadside attraction kitsch for the formula that once brought families to Western North Carolina's theme parks.

Fans of the parks that dotted the hills—Ghost Town in the Sky (Maggie Valley), Frontier Land (Cherokee) and Gold City (Franklin), to name a few—remember the draw, that mix of fun and oddness. The themes varied—from Santa's North Pole to Wild West shootouts—and some were short-lived, but the nostalgia factor remained strong.

Most of the attractions no longer operate, but Tweetsie Railroad (between Boone and Blowing Rock) still chugs out of the station. Just as it did on opening day in 1957, the train is pulled by a real steam engine that once ran regular routes between Boone and eastern Tennessee.

The Wicked Witch's house at the Land of Oz. *Photo by Cathy Pickens.*

Tweetsie's sister park, the Land of Oz (Beech Mountain), closed in 1980, after operating only ten years. Unlike Tweetsie and Ghost Town with their rides and hourly shows, Oz used live actors and took visitors through replicas of movie scenes, starting in Auntie Em's farmhouse, with a crazy-house experience of tilted floors and loud wind to simulate the tornado, before a trip down the Yellow Brick Road. A real-life Dorothy in a blue gingham dress and sparkling red slippers led the way for visitors. The witch's castle was, of course, the scariest stop.

In 1975, thieves first struck Oz, stealing key pieces from the collection of movie memorabilia and setting fire to the theater and shop. When the park closed its gates for good five years later, vandals and souvenir hunters snuck in and damaged many of the sets.

Opposite: A little Dorothy travels the Yellow Brick Road at the Land of Oz. *Courtesy of Bambi Pig via flickr.com.*

Above: The Tin Woodman at the Land of Oz. *Photo by Cathy Pickens.*

In the early 1990s, Cindy Keller and her husband came to Oz. Her day job was to market land development for the property owners, but she also became the unofficial head guardian of Oz.

The Yellow Brick Road, which runs one third of a mile through the stage scenes, was a key feature of the Land of Oz. But souvenir thieves stole some of the original specially made baked-glaze bricks. The replacement bricks lack the glaze and now must be regularly repainted. In a 2015 article, *Charlotte Observer* reporter Mark Washburn interviewed Cindy Keller about the Facebook-fueled craze of investigating "abandoned" sites. Keller works to get the word to college students at nearby Appalachian State and Lees-McRae and others that the site is anything but abandoned, especially for Keller and a loyal group of park fans.

Starting in 1988, a group of Ozzies—some who acted in roles at the park or who just loved the experience—have come together to keep part of it alive, touching up the paint, refreshing the structures for private tours and offering weekend open houses on select dates in fall and summer. (See https://www.landofoznc.com for more information. Tickets sell fast.)

Except as the setting for the castle of the Wicked Witch of the West, mountains didn't play a role in the original *The Wizard of Oz*. After all, Dorothy was from Kansas. But in a region of oddity and mystery, the Land of Oz fits nicely.

REFERENCES

The Mayberry Bombings

Daily Times-News (Burlington, NC). "SBI Confident Bomb Murder Case Solved." April 10, 1954, 1.

Hirsch, Richard. "Postmarked for Prison: Behind the Scenes with the U.S. Postal Inspectors." *True Detective* (February 1941): 56–59, 107–8, 110–11.

Joyce, Tom. "'Mayberry' No Stranger to Horrific Crimes." *Mount Airy News*, May 14, 2016. https://www.mtairynews.com/opinion/40695/mayberry-no-stranger-to-horrific-crimes.

Perry, Thomas D. "Deadly Dentist" and "Mount Airy's Franklin Street Bomber." In *Murder in a Rear View Mirror.* Ararat, VA: Laurel Hill Publishing, 2018, 72–93, 174–85.

Smith, Donna G. "A Bomb for the Bridegroom." In *Murder in Mayberry: True Crime in America's Hometown.* N.p.: privately published, 2012, 67–74.

Suffolk News-Herald. "Edward Banner Is Not to Be Tried on Federal Charges." October 22, 1936, 1. https://virginiachronicle.com.

Long Unsolved

The VISTA Murder

Charlotte Observer. "Young Teacher Found Shot to Death in Sylva." September 16, 1971, 1C.

———. "Youths Saw Girl, Three Companions." June 19, 1970, 1B.

Daily Times-News (Burlington, NC). "Teacher Is Convicted of Murder at Sylva." March 8, 1972.

Dornfried, Joseph. "State v. Johnson: Taking a Strong Stance Against Murder by Poison in North Carolina." 65 N.C. L. Rev. 1231 (1987). http://scholarship.law.unc.edu/nclr/vol65/iss6/12.

Pinsky, Mark I. *Met Her on the Mountain.* Winston-Salem, NC: John F. Blair, 2013. Updated 2021 and published by University Press of Kentucky, 2022.

———. "An Unsolved Murder, a Closed Mountain Community, and a Reporter." Four-part series. *Charlotte Observer*, March 1–4, 2014. https://www.charlotteobserver.com/news/local/crime/article9101153.html#storylink=cpy.

State v. Barnwell, 194 S.E.2d 63 (N.C. App., 1973).

State v. Johnson, 344 S.E.2d 775 (1986).

The Boone Bathtub Murders

Birt, Billy Stonewall. *Rock Solid: The True Story of Georgia's Dixie Mafia.* N.p.: privately published, 2017.

Bullard, Tim. "Cold Case." *Yes! Weekly*, October 17, 2007. http://www.yesweekly.com/article-4121-cold-case.html.

Capuzzo, Michael. *The Murder Room: The Heirs of Sherlock Holmes Gather to Solve the World's Most Perplexing Problems.* New York: Gotham Books, 2010.

Hubbard, Jule. "Perpetrators in Durham Murders Named." *Wilkes Journal-Patriot* (North Wilkesboro), February 12, 2022. https://www.journalpatriot.com/news/perpetrators-in-durham-murders-named/article_5395df29-c5e3-5ef4-95c3-a702fdfa0546.html.

Mitchell, Monte. "40-Year-Old Unsolved Triple Murder Still Haunts Law Enforcement." *Winston-Salem Journal*, February 3, 2012, updated April 16, 2021. https://journalnow.com/40-year-old-unsolved-triple-murder-still-haunts-law-enforcement/article_3f04e50f-a3a2-5aed-9dfb-c0118871ac34.html.

Thompson, Jim. "Billy Sunday Birt, Reputed Mass Murderer and Member of 'Dixie Mafia,' Dies in Prison." *Athens Banner-Herald*, April 17, 2017. https://www.onlineathens.com/story/news/state/2017/04/07/billy-sunday-birt-reputed-mass-murderer-and-member-dixie-mafia-dies-prison/985437007.

The Vidocq Society. https://www.vidocq.org.

Watauga Democrat. "Investigation of Durham Family's Slaying Continues." January 31, 2015. https://www.wataugademocrat.com/news/investigation-of-durham-family-s-slaying-continues/article_e16a2616-a983-11e4-9e07-bbfdbdd91c44.html.

Wise, D.V. "50-Year-Old NC Murder Solved After Augusta Inmate Confesses." WJBF Channel 6, February 9, 2022. https://www.wjbf.com/news/50-year-old-nc-murder-solved-after-augusta-inmate-confesses.

Murder in China

Mann, Jim. "Safety Assumptions in Doubt: Unsolved China Murder Troubles U.S. Educators." *Los Angeles Times*, March 25, 1988. https://www.latimes.com/archives/la-xpm-1988-03-25-mn-296-story.html.

Wilson, Chip. "Who Was the Killer? China Mystery Lingers." *Charlotte Observer*, March 25, 1988, 1C.

Unsolved Mountaintop Murder / Cold Case Solved

Hawks, Stacy N. *Dividing Ridge: The Unsolved Murder of Elva Brannock*. Sparta, NC: Dividing Ridge Books, 2019.

Hewlett, Michael. "Conviction in Cold Case: Guilty Plea in Rape and Murder of 14-Year-Old Rural Hall Girl." *Winston-Salem Journal*, December 17, 2020. https://journalnow.com/news/local/crime-and-courts/conviction-in-cold-case-guilty-plea-in-rape-and-murder-of-14-year-old-rural/article_c95d68fe-40bc-11eb-ae54-2f34013c7e6d.html.

Joyce, Tom. "Dobson Man Sentenced in Cold Case Murder." *Mount Airy News*, January 3, 2021. https://www.mtairynews.com/news/93226/dobson-man-sentenced-in-cold-case-murder.

Linville, Jeff. "Surry Sheriff's Office Cracks Blaylock Cold Case, Makes Arrest." *Mount Airy News*, August 2, 2019. https://www.mtairynews.com/news/76368/surry-sheriffs-office-cracks-blaylock-cold-case-makes-arrest.

"Ronda Blaylock Homicide Task Force" Facebook page. https://www.facebook.com/Ronda-Blaylock-Homicide-Task-Force-783832031705250.

Statesville Record & Landmark. "Blame Liquor in Murder of Girl: Aroused Citizens Cause Four Distilleries to Be Wiped Out in the Section Where Elva Brannock Was Assaulted and Murdered on Way to School." February 22, 1937, 6.

MISSING

Dennis Martin/Trenny Gibson/Polly Melton/Sherry Hart

Baldwin, Juanitta, and Ester Grubb. *Unsolved Disappearances in the Great Smoky Mountains.* Virginia Beach, VA: Suntop Press, 1998, 2001.

Bradley, Michael. *Death in the Great Smoky Mountains: Stories of Accidents and Foolhardiness in the Most Popular Park.* Guilford, CT: Lyons Press, 2016.

The Charley Project. "Thelma Pauline 'Polly' Melton." https://charleyproject.org/case/thelma-pauline-melton.

Koester, Robert J. *Lost Person Behavior: A Search and Rescue Guide on Where to Look—for Land, Air and Water.* Charlottesville, VA: dbS Productions, 2008.

Lakin, Matt. "Missing in the Smokies: Dennis Martin's Disappearance Still Haunts Park 50 Years Later." *USA Today*, June 12, 2019, 1A.

Matheny, Jim. "Dennis Martin Mystery: 50 Years of Life-Saving Lessons." WBIR News 10 Knoxville, April 26, 2019. https://www.wbir.com/article/news/dennis-martin-mystery-50-years-of-life-saving-lessons/51-36c9417f-e7b3-4dd3-a076-780225328f3a.

Sexton, Scott. "Rumors that Her Mother's Killer Remains Free 30 Years After Escaping from Jail Haunt Woman." *Winston-Salem Journal*, February 15, 2015. https://www.journalnow.com/news/columnists/scott_sexton/rumors-that-her-mother-s-killer-remains-free-years-after/article_04a84ea1-0f61-5bcb-80bd-00fde99afa2e.html.

"Sherry Lyall Hart" Facebook page. https://www.facebook.com/sherrylyallhart.

Intentionally Missing

Baker, KC. "Woman Who Was Adopted as Child Learns Biological Dad Is Alleged Killer on FBI's Most Wanted List." *People*, March 9, 2021.

https://people.com/crime/woman-who-was-adopted-as-child-learns-biological-dad-is-alleged-killer-on-fbis-most-wanted-list/?did=613481-20210309&utm_campaign=true-crime_newsletter&utm_source=people.com&utm_medium=email&utm_content=030921&cid=613481&mid=52659317470.

Boerema, Jurgen. "The Bradford Bishop Mystery." *Washington Daily News*, April 11, 2014. https://www.thewashingtondailynews.com/2014/04/11/the-bradford-bishop-mystery.

Federal Bureau of Investigation. "FBI Wanted Poster for William Bradford Bishop Jr." https://www.fbi.gov/wanted/murders/william-bradford-bishop-jr.

Gillcrist, Kathy. *It's In My Genes*. Carolina Shores, NC: Pulse, 2020.

Pigeon Forge. "Explore the Elkmont Ghost Town." August 17, 2020. https://www.pigeonforge.com/elkmont-ghost-town.

Bad Men

The Ore Knob Mine Murders

Haynes, Rose M. *The Ore Knob Murders: The Crimes, the Investigation and the Trials*. Jefferson, NC: McFarland, 2013.

Lehr, Dick, Mitchell Zuckoff and Shelley Murphy. "Whitey and the FBI." Five-part series, starting July 19, 1998. https://archive.boston.com/news/packages/whitey/globe_stories/1998/whitey_and_the_fbi_part_1_0719.htm.

New York Times. "U.S. Agency Links STP Hallucinogen to Mescaline Drug." June 30, 1967.

Rhyne, Nancy. *More Murder in the Carolinas*. John F. Blair: Winston-Salem, NC, 1990, 89–103.

Curtis Shedd

Daily Record (Dunn, NC). "Murderers Die in Gas Chamber." March 23, 1951, 1.

Morrow, Jason Lucky. "Triple-Slayer Curtis Shedd, 1950." *Historical Crime Detective*, blog. https://www.historicalcrimedetective.com/triple-slayer-curtis-shedd-1950.

Reynolds, T.W. *The Southern Appalachian Region: Hitherto Untold Stories*. Vol. 2. N.p.: privately published, 1966, 5–6.

Sylva (NC) Herald & Ruralite. "Jackson County Jury Drawn to Hear Shedd Murder Trial in Macon: N.C. and Georgia Officers Tell of 'Confession.'" December 7, 1950.

———. "S.C. Man's Execution for Slaying Two Girls Set for January 26." December 14, 1950, 18.

The Moonshiners

Hutcheson, Neal. *The Moonshiner Popcorn Sutton.* N.p.: privately published, January 2021.

Johnson, Becky. "Moonshiner Dead in Apparent Suicide." *Smoky Mountain News*, March 18, 2009. https://smokymountainnews.com/archives/item/2651-moonshiner-dead-in-apparent-suicide.

Markovich, Jeremy. "How a Tar Heel Moonshiner Got Away with Murder (in 1892)." *Our State*, May 1, 2018. https://www.ourstate.com/how-a-tar-heel-moonshiner-got-away-with-murder-in-1892.

North Carolina General Statutes 15A-726. "Extradition of Persons Not Present in Demanding State at Time of Commission of Crime." 1937.

State v. Hall, 19 S.E. 602 (N.C. April 1894).

State v. Hall, 20 S.E. 729 (N.C. December 1894).

Sutton, Popcorn. *Me and My Likker: The True Story of a Mountain Moonshiner.* Rev. ed. N.p.: privately published, January 1, 2009.

World of Speed. "From Moonshine to NASCAR: How the Prohibition Lead to Stock Car Racing." December 26, 2019. https://www.worldofspeed.org/archive-blog-1/2019/12/26/from-moonshine-to-nascar.

The Murder Ballads

Tom Dula

Flanders, Judith. *The Invention of Murder: How the Victorians Revelled in Death and Detection and Created Modern Crime.* London: Harper Press, 2011.

State v. Dula, 61 N.C. 211 (1867).

State v. Dula, 61 N.C. 437 (1868).

Underwood, Richard H. *CrimeSong: True Crime Stories from Southern Murder Ballads.* Lexington, KY: Shadelandhouse Modern Press, 2016.

Frankie Silver

Haines, Don. "Tragic Ends: Frankie and Charlie Silver." *Blue Ridge Country*, July 1, 2001. https://blueridgecountry.com/archive/favorites/frankie-and-charlie-silver.

State v. Silver, 14 N.C. 332 (1832).

Young, Perry Deane. *The Untold Story of Frankie Silver*. Bloomington: iUniverse, 2012. Originally published ASJA Press, 1998.

Omie Wise

Grimes, William. "Doc Watson, Blind Guitar Wizard Who Influenced Generations, Dies at 89." *New York Times*, May 30, 2012, A21. https://www.nytimes.com/2012/05/30/arts/music/doc-watson-folk-musician-dies-at-89.html.

Roote, Robert. "The Historical Events Behind the Celebrated Ballad 'Naomi Wise.'" *North Carolina Folklore Journal* 32, no. 2 (Fall/Winter 1984): 70–81.

Schechter, Harold. "The Murder of Omie Wise, 1808." *Yale Review*, June 29, 2018. https://yalereview.org/article/murder-omie-wise-1808.

Oma Hicks

Asheville Citizen-Times. "Parker Naylor Mystery Case Is Near Solution." April 19, 1931, 1.

Big Bend Killing: The Appalachian Ballad Tradition. Album liner notes, accessed via ISSUU. https://issuu.com/greatsmokymountainsassociation/docs/big_bend_liner_notes.

Dean, Nadia. *Murder in the Mountains: Historic True Crime in Western North Carolina*. Cherokee, NC: Valley River Press, 2021.

Find A Grave. "Benjamin Parker 'Ben' Naillon, 1876–1916." https://www.findagrave.com/memorial/67581142/benjamin-parker-naillon.

Statesville Record & Landmark. "Three Men Enter Pleas of Guilty." July 23, 1931, 4. https://www.newspapers.com/clip/2899091/murder-of-scott-brown.

The Asheville Cases

Helen Clevenger

Brown v. Mississippi, 297 U.S. 278 (1936).

Krajicek, David J. "NYU Student's Killer Rushed to Execution in Just 5 Months in 1936." *New York Daily News*, July 30, 2017. https://www. nydailynews.com/news/crime/nyu-student-killer-rushed-execution-5-months-1936-article-1.3368737.

———. "Snagged by a Cord in Killing of Novelist." *New York Daily News*, October 31, 2009. https://www.nydailynews.com/news/crime/snagged-cord-killing-novelist-article-1.418391.

Manikowski, Amy C. "Murder at the Battery Park." *Asheville Historic Inns*, blog, September 2, 2017. https://ashevillehistoricinns.wordpress. com/2017/09/02/murder-at-the-battery-park.

Smith, Anne Chesky. *Murder at Asheville's Battery Park Hotel: The Search for Helen Clevenger's Killer*. Charleston, SC: The History Press, 2021.

Wilson, Colin. *Murder in the 1930s*. New York: Carroll & Graf, 1992, 250–55.

Will Harris Shooting Spree and Thomas Wolfe

Haste, Steve. *Criminal Sentences: True Crime in Fiction and Drama*. London: Cygnus Arts, 1997, 135–36.

Los Angeles Herald. "Posse Kills Murderer Harris." Via Associated Press, November 16, 1906. https://cdnc.ucr.edu/cgi-bin/cdnc?a=d&d= LAH19061116.2.170&e=-------en--20--1--txt-txIN--------1.

Wolfe, Thomas. "The Child by Tiger." *Saturday Evening Post*, September 11, 1937.

The Biltmore Library

Brown, Tony. "Plea Filed; Rare Books Recovered." *Asheville Citizen-Times*, January 13, 1981, 2.

Milling, Marla Hardee. "A Real-Life Biltmore Mystery." *Blue Ridge Country*, July/August 2017. https://blueridgecountry.com/newsstand/magazine/ real-life-biltmore-mystery.

Mountaineers and Rangers: A History of Federal Forest Management in the Southern Appalachians, 1900–81. Chapter 2, "National Forests Organized in Southern Appalachians." National Park Service. http://npshistory.com/publications/usfs/region/8/history/chap2.htm.

Stark, Craig. "George Vanderbilt's Library: A Dream Realized." *Book Think* no. 72 (July 10, 2006). https://www.bookthink.com/0072/72gwv1.htm.

HEADLINE CASES

Missing Hikers and a Serial Killer

Boone, Christopher. "Killer Gary Hilton May Be Linked to Missing Miami Woman." *Atlanta Journal-Constitution*, September 16, 2009. https://www.ajc.com/news/local/killer-gary-hilton-may-linked-missing-miami-woman/o5EYtdPxT9VDfwarP21txL.

Butcher, Lee. *At the Hands of a Stranger.* New York: Pinnacle Books, 2012.

Cagle, John. *Those Days in January: The Abduction and Murder of Meredith Hope Emerson.* Alpharetta, GA: BookLogix, 2020.

Dressler, Jacob. "Deadly Run: The Horror Movie a Real Serial Killer Helped Create." ScreenGeek, April 17, 2020. https://www.screengeek.net/2020/04/17/deadly-run-movie-real-serial-killer.

Harrell, Michelle, Melissa Register and Billy Zakrzewski. "Gary Michael Hilton." Department of Psychology, Radford University, Radford, Virginia. http://maamodt.asp.radford.edu/Psyc%20405/serial%20killers/Hilton,%20Gary%20Michael.pdf.

Jones, Erica. "12 Years After Emerson Murder, Lead Investigator Releases Tell-All Book." *Dawson (GA) News*, March 18, 2020. https://www.dawsonnews.com/local/12-years-after-emerson-murder-lead-investigator-releases-tell-all-book.

Strange Outdoors. "The Strange Disappearance of Jason Knapp from Table Rock State Park." November 6, 2017. https://www.strangeoutdoors.com/mysterious-stories-blog/jason-knapp.

Williams, Mike. "Tragic End for 'Unique Couple.'" *Atlanta Journal-Constitution*, June 21, 2011. https://www.ajc.com/news/local/tragic-end-for-unique-couple/PzAHQbeBqHLPzNjGei0nAJ.

Eric Rudolph

Federal Bureau of Investigation. "Eric Rudolph." FBI's Famous Crimes & Criminals. https://www.fbi.gov/history/famous-cases/eric-rudolph.

Hager, Eli. "My Life in the Supermax." Interview with Travis Dusenbury. The Marshall Project, in collaboration with *Vice*, January 8, 2016. https://www.themarshallproject.org/2016/01/08/my-life-in-the-supermax.

Lewis, Cynthia. "Whatever Happened to the Search for Eric Rudolph?" *Southern Cultures* 7, no. 4 (Winter 2001): 5–30. https://www.southerncultures.org/article/whatever-happened-search-eric-rudolph.

Markovich, Jeremy. "Here's What Happened to the Rookie NC Officer Who Nabbed Bomber Eric Rudolph." *Our State* and WFAE, December 3, 2019. https://www.wfae.org/local-news/2019-12-03/heres-what-happened-to-the-rookie-nc-officer-who-nabbed-bomber-eric-rudolph#stream/0.

Morrison, Blake. "Special Report: Eric Rudolph." Two-part series. *USA Today*, July 5–6, 2005. https://usatoday30.usatoday.com/news/nation/2005-07-05-rudolph-cover-partone_x.htm.

The Pisgah Inn Murder

Drew, Jonathan. "A Central Florida Woman Was Killed While Working a Summer Job in N.C. Her Last Words: 'This Is a Safe Place.'" *Orlando Sentinel*, via Associated Press, July 27, 2018. https://www.orlandosentinel.com/news/breaking-news/os-sara-ellis-killed-north-carolina-20180727-story.html.

Wicker, Mackenzie. "Pendergraft Sentenced to Multiple Life Terms in Prison for Pisgah Inn Murder." *Asheville Citizen-Times*, February 27, 2020. https://www.citizen-times.com/story/news/local/2020/02/27/derek-pendergraft-sentenced-life-prison-pisgah-inn-murder/4881583002.

SIDE TRIPS, CRIME BITS AND ODDITIES

Graveyard Rabbits

Cross, Tom Peete. "Witchcraft in North Carolina." *Studies in Philology* 16, no. 3 (July 1919): 217–87. https://www.jstor.org/stable/4171754.

Harris, Joel Chandler. "A Phantom Witch." Uncle Remus. https://www.uncleremus.com/plantationwitch.html.

Stanton, Frank Lebby. "The Graveyard Rabbit." All Poetry. https://allpoetry.com/The-Graveyard-Rabbit.

Sylva's Goat Gland Doctor

Brock, Pope. *Charlatan: America's Most Dangerous Huckster, the Man Who Pursued Him, and the Age of Flimflam.* New York: Crown Publishers, 2008.

Elliston, Jon. "Bad Medicine: The Remarkable Rise and Fall of the Goat Gland King, Jackson County's 'Dr.' John Brinkley." *WNC Magazine* (January/February 2017). https://wncmagazine.com/feature/bad_medicine.

Fowler, Hayley. "'Goat Gland King' Conned Impotent Men Across the US." *Charlotte Observer*, July 8, 2021. https://www.charlotteobserver.com/news/state/north-carolina/article252650178.html#storylink=cp.

Schruben, Francis W. "The Wizard of Milford: Dr. J.R. Brinkley and Brinkleyism." *Kansas History* 14, no. 4 (Winter 1991/1992): 226. https://www.kshs.org/publicat/history/1991winter_schruben.pdf.

Other Cases

Cashiers Historical Society. *Historical Sites Survey, Phase I*, 2011. https://issuu.com/cashiershs/docs/chs_surveybook_2011.

Elliston, Jon. "Theme Park Land: Western North Carolina's Worlds of Wonder." *WNC Magazine* (Summer 2021). https://wncmagazine.com/feature/theme_park_land.

Ferguson, Stuart. "Whodunnit—Highlands Style." *Laurel Magazine* (July 7, 2021). https://www.thelaurelmagazine.com/arts-in-highlands-nc-and-cashiers-nc/whodunnit-highlands-style.

Nardy, Jane Gibson. "Shots Rang Out in Cashiers NC." *Laurel Magazine* (Winter 2018). https://www.thelaurelmagazine.com/history-in-highlands-nc-and-cashiers-nc/shots-rang-out-in-cashiers-nc.

Reynolds, T.W. *High Lands*. N.p.: privately published, 1964, 7, 158.

Warren, Joshua. *Brown Mountain Lights: A Viewing Guide*. Shadowbox Enterprises. http://shadowboxent.brinkster.net/bml%20viewing%20guide_9-16-13.pdf.

Washburn, Mark. "Some Enchanted Thieving." *Charlotte Observer*, June 14, 2015, 1A.

WCNC News. "Drive Into the Paranormal in the Blue Ridge Mountains." October 24, 2016. https://www.wcnc.com/article/news/crime/drive-into-the-paranormal-in-the-blue-ridge-mountains/340677859.

ABOUT THE AUTHOR

C athy Pickens, a lawyer and college professor, is a crime fiction writer (*Southern Fried Mysteries*, St. Martin's/Minotaur) and true crime columnist for *Mystery Readers Journal*. She is professor emerita in the McColl School of Business and served as national president of Sisters in Crime and on the boards of Mystery Writers of America and the Mecklenburg Forensic Medicine Program (an evidence collection/ preservation training collaborative). She is also the author of *CREATE!* (ICSC Press), offers coaching and workshops on developing the creative process and works with writers on telling their stories.

Other books from Cathy Pickens and The History Press include:

Charleston Mysteries
Charlotte True Crime Stories
Triangle True Crime Stories
True Crime Stories of Eastern North Carolina
True Crime Stories of Upstate South Carolina